Collins

Cambridge Lower Secondary

English

PROGRESS BOOK STAGE 7: STUDENT'S BOOK

Series editors: Julia Burchell and Mike Gould
Authors: Julia Burchell and Mike Gould

William Collins' dream of knowledge for all began with the publication of his first book in 1819.
A self-educated mill worker, he not only enriched millions of lives, but also founded a flourishing publishing house.
Today, staying true to this spirit, Collins books are packed with inspiration, innovation and practical expertise.
They place you at the centre of a world of possibility and give you exactly what you need to explore it.

Collins. Freedom to teach.

Published by Collins

An imprint of HarperCollins*Publishers*
The News Building, 1 London Bridge Street, London, SE1 9GF, UK

HarperCollins*Publishers*
Macken House, 39/40 Mayor Street Upper, Dublin 1, D01 C9W8, Ireland

Browse the complete Collins catalogue at
collins.co.uk

10 9 8 7 6 5 4 3 2 1

ISBN 978-0-00-865503-7

British Library Cataloguing-in-Publication Data
A catalogue record for this publication is available from the British Library.

The questions, worked examples, accompanying marks and mark schemes included in this resource have been written by the authors and are for guidance only. They do not replicate examination papers and the questions in this resource will not appear in your exams. In examinations the way marks are awarded may be different. Any references to assessment and/or assessment preparation are the authors' interpretation of the syllabus requirements.

Whilst every attempt to ensure that advice on the qualification and its assessment is accurate, the official syllabus and specimen assessment materials are the only authoritative source of information and should always be referred to for definitive guidance.

This text has not been through the Cambridge International endorsement process.

Series editors: Julia Burchell and Mike Gould
Authors: Julia Burchell and Mike Gould
Product manager: Catherine Martin
Development editor: Judith Walters
Copyeditor: Catherine Dakin
Proofreader: Claire Throp
Text permissions researcher: Rachel Thorne
Cover designer: Gordon McGilp
Cover illustrator: Ann Paganuzzi
Typesetter: David Jimenez
Production controller: Alhady Ali
Printed and bound by Martins the Printers

Introduction

Welcome to the Collins Cambridge Lower Secondary English Progress Book 7 Student's Book. We hope it will support you to secure your skills and understanding, and to track your progress through the Cambridge Lower Secondary course.

The Progress Book is made up of the following types of support.

Securing skills

The securing skills units provide extra practice and guidance to help consolidate the most important skills from each chapter of the Collins *Cambridge Lower Secondary Stage 7* Student's Book (ISBN 9780008340834).

They are designed to help you feel confident that you are mastering the objectives in each strand of the Cambridge Lower Secondary English curriculum framework. They could be completed while you work through the Student's Book chapter. Alternatively, you could use them after your final tasks in the Student's Book chapter have been assessed by your teacher, to target particular skills.

Tests

The Progress Book also contains three tests on non-fiction and three on fiction (including poetry and drama).

Each pair of tests could be tackled after you have completed two consecutive chapters of the Student's Book, as they give you the opportunity to apply skills you have been developing in those chapters and to practise answering a range of questions. They will help you to understand what you are doing well and where you may need further support.

Each test is subdivided into a reading and writing section. The texts chosen for the reading section correspond with the focus of the relevant Student's Book chapter. For Stage 7 these are Describing, Informing, Advising and persuading, Narrating, Reviewing and discussing, and Exploring and commenting. You will be asked to produce your own piece of writing for the same purpose in the writing section of the test.

Suggested timings have been included for each test. In Stage 7, these timings give you more time for reading and planning. This time will be reduced as you move into Stages 8 and 9.

The skills tested are identified on the self-assessment feedback sheets. Here you or your teacher can record your marks, and you can then review your performance to pinpoint where you have done well and where you feel less confident. There is space for you to set yourself goals for further study.

End of year assessments

At the end of the book, you will find two end of year assessments, one based on a non-fiction text and one on a fiction extract. Each assessment is then subdivided into reading and writing sections. These assessments are intended to be used at the end of the stage or school year, drawing together all the learning from the stage or year. These assessments give you an opportunity to practise a more formal assessment, under timed conditions, to help you prepare for external or internal assessment at the end of Lower Secondary.

Again, feedback sheets are provided to help you reflect on your progress.

Answers

Answers to each securing skills unit, test and end of year assessment are available by request from www.collins.co.uk/internationalresources.

Chapter 1: Understanding how writers create descriptions

These tasks will help you secure the following skills from Chapter 1 of the Student's Book:
- understand the elements which make up a description
- understand how writers use imagery, and precise adverbs and adjectives for effect.

Read the following extract from the novel *Jamaica Inn* by Daphne du Maurier. The novel is set in a time when long distance travel was often in a shared, horse-drawn carriage called a coach.

> It was a cold grey day in late November. The weather had changed overnight, when a **backing** wind brought a granite sky and a **mizzling** rain with it, and although it was now only a little after two o'clock in the afternoon the pallor of a winter evening seemed to have closed upon the hills, cloaking them in mist. It would be dark by four. The air was clammy cold, and for all the tightly closed windows it penetrated the interior of the coach. The leather seats felt damp to the hands, and there must have been a small crack in the roof, because now and again little drips of rain fell softly through, smudging the leather and leaving a dark blue stain like a splodge of ink.
>
> The wind came in gusts, at times shaking the coach as it travelled round the bend of the road, and in the exposed places on the high ground it blew with such force that the whole body of the coach trembled and swayed, rocking between the high wheels [...].
>
> The driver, muffled in a greatcoat to his ears, bent almost double in his seat, in a faint endeavour to gain shelter from his own shoulders, while the dispirited horses plodded sullenly to his command, too broken by the wind and the rain to feel the whip that now and again cracked above their heads, while it swung between the numb fingers of the driver.
>
> From *Jamaica Inn* by Daphne du Maurier

(line references: 5, 10, 15)

Vocabulary

backing: cold

mizzling: slight

1   This extract contains all the 'ingredients' for a piece of description.
    Complete the table below, identifying the details du Maurier uses in each category.

Time of year		Objects/Animals/People	
Time of day		Movement	
Weather		Sounds/Smells/Tastes	
General landscape		Colours	
Textures	Damp seats		

2 A feature of descriptions is that they are written to help the reader imagine that they are present at the scene. This writer uses adjectives and adverbs to convey a precise experience of the scene.

a Copy out three phrases where the writer does this.

A _____

B _____

C _____

b Select **one** of the three phrases from part **a** and explain exactly what the adverb or adjective used means.

Phrase A/B/C:

Meaning of adjective or adverb:

_____

_____

c How does this adjective or adverb help you to imagine the scene more clearly? Tick one or more of the following ways it might help.

It helps me to *see*. ☐

It helps me to *hear*. ☐

It helps me to *feel*. ☐

3 Writers also use comparisons to help us to imagine. Explain how the writer uses a simile to help us to see the shape of the stain made by the drip of water in the first paragraph.

The writer compares the stain made by the drip to _____

which makes us think that the stain is _____.

_____

4 Now write your own paragraph explaining how the writer helps you to imagine that you are present on the coach.

_____

_____

_____

_____

_____

_____

_____

Chapter 1: Understanding how writers create atmosphere

These tasks will help you secure the following skills from Chapter 1 of the Student's Book:
• understand how language and literary techniques create atmosphere
• analyse how effects are created by writing a structured paragraph.

Read this extract from the novel *Jamaica Inn* by Daphne du Maurier (also used on pages 6–7).

> The wheels of the coach creaked and groaned as they sank into the ruts on the road, and sometimes they flung up the soft spattered mud against the windows, where it mingled with the constant driving rain, and whatever view there might have been of the countryside was hopelessly obscured.
>
> The few passengers huddled together for warmth, exclaiming in unison when the coach sank into a heavier rut than usual, and one old fellow, who had kept up a constant complaint ever since he had joined the coach at Truro, rose from his seat in a fury, and, fumbling with the window sash, let the window down with a crash, bringing a shower of rain in upon himself and his fellow passengers.
>
> From *Jamaica Inn* by Daphne du Maurier

5

Writers often use words with connotations to create a mood or atmosphere in a description.

1 The coach wheels are described as having 'groaned'.

   a What are the usual connotations of this word?

   _____

   _____

   b Why do you think the writer chose this word?

   _____

   _____

2 Copy out **three** words or phrases from the second paragraph that suggest that the coach journey is not comfortable for the passengers.

   A _____

   B _____

   C _____

3 The paragraphs in the extract contain a variety of sounds. Look closely at those made by the coach and the passengers. Tick the statement below that best describes the atmosphere that these descriptions create.

   A The wheels and the people are unhappy. ☐

   B 'Groaned' and 'exclaiming' suggest that both the coach and the people are in discomfort. ☐

   C The coach seems dominated by a negative atmosphere. ☐

4 Look again at the table from task 1 on page 6. Using what you now know about the extract, note down the atmosphere that you think is created by each of the ingredients.

Ingredient	Atmosphere created	Ingredient	Atmosphere created
Time of year		Objects/Animals/People	
Time of day	Unease as it is dark.	Movement	
Weather		Sounds/Smells/Tastes	
General landscape		Colours	
Textures			

5 Use a simple structure to write a paragraph explaining how the writer creates a sense of negativity in this extract.

State a clear idea about what the writer has done in the text.

For example:

The writer has made the journey seem extremely uncomfortable by describing the movement of the carriage...

Support your idea with a quotation as evidence.

For example:

...using verbs such as 'swayed' and 'rocking'.

Explain how specific features of the quotation help you to sense the atmosphere. Comment on the precise meaning of words, their connotations and structure, use of imagery and the sensory picture created.

For example:

The precise meanings of these words tells us that the carriage is moving a lot from side to side, which might make the passengers and driver feel very uncomfortable and maybe unwell.

_____

_____

_____

_____

_____

_____

_____

_____

Chapter 1: Writing to create a sense of place

These tasks will help you secure the following skills from Chapter 1 of the Student's Book:
- choose precise adjectives and adverbs to provide detail and create atmosphere
- use imagery and words with particular associations for effect
- avoid duplication by using synonyms and pronouns.

A good description needs to cover a range of details about a place. Before you start writing, make some broad choices, then go into more detail. Remember that before you start, you should decide what atmosphere you want to create as this will influence your choices.

1   Think about a description of an afternoon in the park.

   a   What atmosphere do you want to create? _____

   b   In the table below, note down your choices for your description.

Time of year		Objects/Animals/People	
Time of day		Movement	
Weather		Sounds/Smells/Tastes	
General landscape		Colours	
Textures			

It is important to *show* rather than tell. How are you going to convey the time of year without naming the season? An easy way to do this is via the weather or general landscape.

2   Read the sentence below.

> Motes of light sparkled on the rippling pond water, reflecting the amber sun scorching down on the lily pads and catching the iridescent dragon-fly wings as they touched down and then took off on the breeze.

   a   In which season could the sentence be set? Explain why you think this.

   _____

   b   Now write your own sentence describing the pond at another time of year.

   _____

   _____

   _____

Varying the words that you use is important in a description; otherwise, it can become repetitive. Using pronouns and synonyms is one way to overcome this problem.

3   Read the description of a waiting room below.

> The grey painted door opened onto a wide, echoing room, more a hallway than a room. Along each of its long sides were rows of chairs with metal legs and large shiny greying plastic cushions. The chairs were crammed in, almost overlapping, with an occasional low table dividing the rows. Every chair wore its battle wounds: a smudge of biro, a scratch, a streak of greying stickiness.

a Underline the repeated words in the description.

b Now rewrite the description so that there are no duplications.

_____

_____

_____

_____

Using precise words and phrases is another way of helping the reader to visualise a scene.

4 Rewrite the following sentences describing a welcoming café, adding in precise adjectives and adverbs to help your reader.

a The café was made of _____ logs, like a cabin out of a snowy movie.

b The _____ windows shone with warm light from within.

c _____ shutters hung to the sides of the doors, ready to keep cold winds out on a blustery day.

d A gorgeous _____ honeysuckle plant wound its way around the doors, wafting its _____ scent to all who brushed past.

Some words have implicit connotations which can add detail to your description.

5 Describe a bird landing on a table at an outdoor café in two different ways.

a First, use words that we associate with soldiers.

_____

_____

_____

b Now rewrite your description using words associated with dance.

_____

_____

_____

Literary devices, such as similes and metaphors, can also add extra detail and atmosphere.

6 Write **two** similes that could be used to describe the way a tree is standing in a garden. Then explain the effect you are creating.

a Simile: _____

Effect: _____

_____

b Simile: _____

Effect: _____

_____

Chapter 2: Identifying information

These tasks will help you secure the following skills from Chapter 2 of the Student's Book:
- skim and scan to locate relevant information
- filter out opinion to find relevant information.

Read the text below.

All you need to know about El Ingenio

Where is it?

The brilliant El Ingenio Shopping Centre is located on the edge of Vélez-Málaga and Torre del Mar, which are 30 minutes east of Malaga.

What does it contain?

The centre is superbly designed in a long, narrow right-angle shape with entrances at either end and cafés at the start, end and in the middle. In fact, there is a huge second floor food court at the cinema end above the wonderful array of shops below.

5

What sort of shops and restaurants does it have?

The two arms of the shopping centre are flanked by zillions of shops of all kinds, from clothes and shoes to a large supermarket, with small, classy boutiques, electronic game stores, jewellers and an adorable babywear outlet competing for your attention, alongside make-up stores, perfumiers and even a shop selling comfy beds! At one end is a mezzanine floor housing a seven-screen cinema and an array of cafés and restaurants accessed by a lift and escalators. From these it is only minutes to all the main fast-food outlets as well as a really fabulous pizzeria, a tapas bar selling a vast array of fresh 'pinchos' and several family-oriented restaurants, including one with an indoor ball pond and climbing area.

10

15

Travelling to the mall

- It is surrounded by parking on three sides: the cinema car park is at the back of the mall with its own entrance, which brings you into the shopping centre at the bottom of the cinema escalators.

20

- There is also a taxi rank outside.

- Buses stop nearby regularly.

Opening hours

Just one word of warning about Sundays, though. I think the mall is only open for a few special Sundays a year (although the cinema is open every day of the week, I believe).

25

---

1 Which presentational features of an information text has the writer used to help you to locate the information that you may need. List **three**.

1 _____

2 _____

3 _____

Skimming a text gives you a rough idea of where to look for specific information.

2   Which paragraph would you go to for information about the types of restaurants that are available at the shopping centre?

_____

Scanning for facts is quick if you decide on a key word to look for.

3   **a**   If you wanted to know whether there were any shops selling baby clothes, what key word would you scan for?

_____

    b   If you wanted to know how many screens the cinema has, what key word would you scan for?

_____

Sometimes you may need to find a synonym, or a word that is closely related to the word that you are looking for.

4   **a**   Imagine that you want to get a coffee at El Ingenio. The word 'coffee' is not in the extract. What other word could you scan for?

_____

    b   Can you get a burger in the food court? The word 'burger' is not in the extract. What other words could you scan for?

_____

Often you will need to filter out unnecessary content, such as opinions, when you are scanning for specific facts or information.

5   Find **three** examples of opinions, adjectives that provide judgments, or exaggerations.

    1   _____

    2   _____

    3   _____

6   Use the strategies above to answer the following questions.

    a   Is El Ingenio open on Sundays? _____

    b   Is there somewhere for children to play while adults eat at the mall? _____

    c   Can you buy perfume at El Ingenio? _____

    d   Can you buy a bottle of milk at the mall? _____

These tasks will help you secure the following skills from Chapter 2 of the Student's Book:
* select information and write notes
* summarise information.

Read the text below that comes from a travel magazine.

COME TO SAL, CAPE VERDE, THE ISLAND THAT'S GOT IT ALL

Everything for Everyone!

Sal island is a short, under five-hour hop from most of mainland Europe and only 350 miles off the West Coast of Africa. Once you are there, you will want for nothing!

Arid and sparsely planted, the island has several unspoilt rocky beaches. (On one of these, you can paddle with baby lemon sharks, if you can stay upright!) The high winds mean that this is a paradise for windsurfers and other adventurous souls. The interior is a red desert scattered with rocks and is fairly inhospitable, so you won't come across much in the way of wildlife! This makes it ideal for wonderfully bumpy, dune buggy excursions (as long as you take plenty of bottled water with you – there is no natural fresh water). Try not to crash either as the nearest major hospital is in Africa! On the edge of the island, several disused saltpans make for a fascinating visit and one even allows you to swim, in a magical floatation experience which rivals the Dead Sea. 5

10

Sal has a gloriously dry tropical climate with the highest rainfall being in August, which is the rainy season. March to June is dry and November to February can be changeable. The temperature peaks in the 30s during the summer and is rarely below 18 even in the winter. The wind is fairly constant! Beware the sun, which is incredibly strong even in the breeze and under the clouds. You shouldn't have any problem as long as you wear sunscreen and pick a sheltered spot. 15

Newer immaculate hotels and accommodation tend to cluster around the coast, although there are a few towns inland where locals tend to live. Resorts offer everything you could need, from food and drink to classes and activities, and are mainly run like a club with everything free to members. Hotels often cater for children: some even have kids clubs, waterparks and play areas. In the capital, Santa Maria, you can eat out and enjoy a variety of restaurants and cafés. There is even an ice-cream parlour! Food and drink can be pricey given that it all has to be brought in by plane or boat, but hey, you're on holiday! 20

25

The island's motto is 'no stress' and it certainly lives up to it!

---

1 Look at these two note-taking tasks. Underline the words that tell you the different focus of each task.

Task 1: Make notes on whether Sal could be a suitable venue for a water sports training camp.

Task 2: Make notes on the main disadvantages of Sal as a place to live.

2 Make notes on whether Sal would be a good holiday destination for:

    a a family with a 12-year-old child

    b a family with a 2-year-old child.

Find the relevant information in the text and write your notes in the table below.

Notes	a Family with 12-year-old child	b Family with 2-year-old child
Pros	under 5-hour hop	
Cons		5-hour hop too long

When you write a summary of a text, you need to use your own words, cut details and examples, and write concisely.

3 Rewrite the following sentence in your own words.

> Newer immaculate hotels and accommodation tend to cluster around the coast, although there are a few towns inland where locals tend to live.

_____

_____

4 Underline the examples in this sentence.

> Hotels often cater for children: some even have kids clubs, waterparks and play areas.

5 Rewrite the following sentence more concisely.

> The interior is a red desert scattered with rocks and is fairly inhospitable, so you won't come across much in the way of wildlife!

_____

_____

6 Imagine that you are selecting a family holiday with a 2-year-old child. Write a summary suggesting that Sal, Cape Verde, would not be a good holiday destination. Write 100 words or fewer.

_____

_____

_____

_____

_____

_____

Chapter 2: Writing informative texts

These tasks will help you secure the following skills from Chapter 2 of the Student's Book:
- select content and features that suit an audience
- write in formal or informal styles to suit an audience.

The intended audience of a text will influence many choices made by the writer. The most fundamental one being what information goes into the text.

1   Imagine that you are creating an informative article about your school for a webpage on secondary school choices in your local area.

   a   Tick who you think is the most likely target audience for this type of text.

   - parents ☐   - pensioners ☐   - 20- to 30-year-old men ☐

   b   What do you think this audience is going to want to know about your school? List five things below.

   1   _____

   2   _____

   3   _____

   4   _____

   5   _____

2   Look at the notepad that includes additional ideas for things to include in your article.

   a   Tick those which you think would be suitable for a target audience of parents.

   b   Now tick those which would be suitable for an audience of students who might be interested in attending the school.

	Parents	Students
Comments about school meals	☐	☐
Photographs of senior teachers	☐	☐
List of uniform	☐	☐
Table of public exam results	☐	☐
Details of any costs	☐	☐
Photographs of school buildings and classrooms	☐	☐
Biographies of teachers with their qualifications	☐	☐
Information about the curriculum covered	☐	☐
List of before/after school clubs and activities	☐	☐
Photographs of uniform	☐	☐
Review of recent school concerts/plays/sport fixtures	☐	☐

Writers are careful to match the level of formality that they use to their audience.

3 a List some types of informal language to be avoided if you were writing the article for parents on secondary school choices.

1 _____

2 _____

3 _____

4 _____

5 _____

b Rewrite the following sentences in a more formal and appropriate style for the webpage aimed at parents.

i Hey! This school is the right place for your kid to be!

_____

ii The teachers have studied hard, by the way, and they know their stuff.

_____

iii The place isn't ready to fall down just yet but there are bits and pieces being done anyway.

_____

Both vocabulary and style need to be matched to the age and education level of readers.

4 Complete the following table, changing each word or phrase to suit the target audience.

Student	Adult
	Curriculum
There's loads to do after school.	
	Uniform requirements

5 You are going to write a 300-word informative blog for a webpage called INSIDE VOICE, which tells new students what to expect when they join your school.

a Plan your content and features:

Content

- What would they like to know?
- What you wish you had known before you came to the school.

Organisation and features

- Page layout, headings, bullets, images, fact boxes…

Vocabulary and style

- What level of formality will you use for this text and audience? What sort of language could you use?

b Write your blog on a separate sheet of paper.

Test 1: NON-FICTION

This test is 90 minutes long (including 30 minutes of reading and planning time).

Section A: Reading

Spend 45 minutes on this section.

*Before you answer the test questions, spend **15 minutes** reading and making notes.*

Read the text extract. It is taken from a webpage that celebrates everything about chocolate.

As you are reading, note down your answers to the big five questions.

- What is the purpose of this text?
- What is the extract about?
- Where is the writer writing about?
- Who do you think this webpage is for?
- Why has the writer written this text?

(These notes are to help you prepare for the test. They will not be given marks.)

What are the Best Cacao Beans in the World?

Have you ever wondered what makes some chocolate bars taste better than others? Many factors influence the final flavor and texture of chocolate, but one of the fundamental elements is the type of cacao beans used to make the chocolate. Cacao beans come in at least ten different varieties with several subvarieties, but most farmers and cultivators consider the three main types to be forastero, criollo and trinitario.

5

So, what are the best cacao beans in the world? Keep reading to find out.

What are the Best Cacao Beans in the World?

Chocolate's story began thousands of years ago in Mesoamerica (present day Central and South America). The first Theobroma (cacao) trees were found over 4,000 years ago in what is now Mexico and Central America.   10

The ancient Olmec people in southeast Mexico were probably the first ones to consume cacao beans. The Aztecs used cacao beans to create a bitter chocolate drink called Xocoatl. This thick, foamy drink was made by grinding roasted cacao beans into a paste that they then mixed with water, vanilla, chili peppers and other spices. The Mayans also used cacao beans as currency and in rituals. These ancient   15 civilizations believed cacao beans were more valuable than gold, and chocolate played an important economic, spiritual and political role in their cultures.

Today, cacao trees are grown around the world in countries with a tropical climate — [in regions] like West Africa, Central and South America and Southeast Asia. In fact, most of the world's cacao beans, around 75 per cent, are currently grown in West Africa.   20

Cacao trees are planted close together under the shelter of taller trees that provide protection from excessive wind and rain. The cacao tree produces a **football-shaped** fruit (or pod) that grows on branches and the trunk and can make up to 2,000 pods per year. Cacao pods are harvested all year long.

What makes cacao beans the best? A variety of factors play a role, including   25
the following:

* **Soil and climate.** The terroir, or environment, influences the final flavor profile of the cacao beans. This includes the nutrients in the soil, the amount of rainfall, the amount of sunlight, wind and temperature.

* **Flavor profile.** The primary flavors of chocolate should include a mix of   30
  bitterness with the right amount of acidity, with fruity, nutty, spicy or floral notes.

* **Processing.** The way cacao beans are processed also influences the final outcome. Cacao beans that are fermented incorrectly, roasted too long or not enough and many other variables all influence the final flavor and texture of the chocolate bar.   35

From the Cococlectic website, 6 September 2023

Vocabulary

football-shaped: the oval shape of an American football

*Spend **30 minutes** on this section.*

1 List **five** features which suggest that this is an information text.

1 *Photo of cacao beans*

2 _____

3 _____

4 _____

5 _____ [2]

2 How many varieties of cacao beans are there?

_____ [1]

3 Where were cacao beans first consumed?

_____ [1]

4 Look at lines 11–12. Which **one** word in the following sentence tells you that this is an opinion, not a fact?

The ancient Olmec people in southeast Mexico were probably the first ones to consume cacao beans.

_____ [1]

5 Look at the fourth paragraph (lines 11–17). Which four-word phrase tells you that cacao beans were important to the Aztecs and Mayans?

_____ [1]

6 Look at the sixth paragraph (lines 21–24). Which **two** words suggest that the cacao trees are fragile?

_____ [2]

7 Why does the writer include figures such as '75 per cent' and '2,000 pods' in the article?

_____ [1]

8 a What type of audience is this text written for? Tick **two** boxes.

- Young children ☐

- People who know quite a bit about chocolate already ☐

- Adults ☐

- People who eat a lot of chocolate ☐ [1]

b Why do you think that?

_____ [1]

9 Look at the following sentence from lines 22–24. Why does the writer use brackets?

The cacao tree produces a football-shaped fruit (or pod) that grows on branches and the trunk and can make up to 2,000 pods per year.

_____ [1]

10 Look at lines 22–23. The writer compares a football and a cocoa pod. Explain why the writer uses this comparison.

_____ [1]

11 Why are bullet points used at the end of the extract?

_____ [1]

12 Look again at the information contained in the first bullet point titled 'Soil and climate' (lines 27–29).

Is the language the writer uses formal or informal? Tick **one** answer.

Formal ☐   Informal ☐   [1]

13 The writer uses questions in several places in the article. Find **two** different examples and explain why each has been used.

Example: _____

Why it is used: _____

Example: _____

Why it is used: _____

[2]

14 Look at lines 33–35. This sentence could be split into several simpler ones. Rewrite it into **three** sentences. (You may add/alter words for fluency.)

Cacao beans that are fermented incorrectly, roasted too long or not enough and many other variables all influence the final flavor and texture of the chocolate bar.

_____

_____

_____ [1]

15 a Does the article suggest that creating the best chocolate is easy?

Y ☐   N ☐   [1]

b Why? Give **two** reasons.

_____

_____

_____ [1]

16 a A journalist visiting Costa Rica to see how the process of making chocolate begins, makes notes during a visit to a plantation. Complete her notes below.

Everything you need to know about where chocolate comes from

History

_____

_____

_____

Proper name

_____

_____

_____

Types

_____

_____

_____

Best way to plant

_____

_____

_____

Preferred weather

_____

_____

_____

[3]

b Using the information in the notebook above, write a summary of up to 50 words about the way that cacao beans should be grown and processed to make chocolate.

_____

_____

_____

_____ [2]

Section B: Writing

*Spend 45 minutes on this section. You may spend **15 minutes** planning your answer below.*

17 Write an encyclopedia entry for an imaginary type of sweet treat. The encyclopedia is aimed at children aged 8–12.

You could include:

- what it is made of

- where some of the ingredients were first discovered

- who first put the ingredients together to make the treat

- why people like it.

Write your plan here.

Write your encyclopedia entry on a separate sheet of paper. [25]

Test 2: FICTION

This test is 90 minutes long (including 30 minutes of reading and planning time).

Section A: Reading

Spend 45 minutes on this section.

*Before you answer the test questions, spend **15 minutes** reading and making notes.*

Read the text extract.

As you are reading, note down your answers to the big five questions.

* Who is the extract about?

* What is happening in the extract?

* When are the events happening: now, in the past or in the future?

* Where do the events take place?

* Why has the writer written this text?

(These notes are to help you prepare for the test. They will not be given marks.)

'An important room, this!' cried Mr Wonka, taking a bunch of keys from his pocket and slipping one into the keyhole of the door. 'This is the nerve centre of the whole factory, the heart of the whole business! And so beautiful! I insist upon my rooms being beautiful! I can't abide ugliness in factories! In we go, then! But do be careful, my dear children! Don't lose your heads! Don't get over-excited! Keep very calm!'   5

Mr Wonka opened the door. Five children and nine grown-ups pushed their ways in — and oh, what an amazing sight it was that now met their eyes!

They were looking down upon a lovely valley. There were green meadows on either side of the valley, and along the bottom of it there flowed a great brown river.

What is more, there was a tremendous waterfall halfway along the river — a steep cliff   10
over which the water curled and rolled in a solid sheet, and then went crashing down into a boiling churning whirlpool of froth and spray.

Below the waterfall (and this was the most astonishing sight of all), a whole mass of enormous glass pipes were dangling down into the river from somewhere high up in the ceiling! They really were enormous, those pipes. There must have been a dozen of   15
them at least, and they were sucking up the brownish muddy water from the river and carrying it away to goodness knows where. And because they were made of glass, you could see the liquid flowing and bubbling along inside them, and above the noise of the waterfall, you could hear the never-ending suck-suck-sucking sound of the pipes as they did their work.   20

Graceful trees and bushes were growing along the riverbanks — weeping willows and alders and tall clumps of rhododendrons with their pink and red and mauve blossoms. In the meadows there were thousands of buttercups.

'There!' cried Mr Wonka, dancing up and down and pointing his gold-topped cane at the great brown river. 'It's all chocolate! Every drop of that river is hot melted chocolate   25
of the finest quality. The very finest quality. There's enough chocolate in there to fill every bathtub in the entire country! And all the swimming pools as well! Isn't it terrific? And just look at my pipes! They suck up the chocolate and carry it away to all the other rooms in the factory where it is needed! Thousands of gallons an hour, my dear children! Thousands and thousands of gallons!'   30

From *Charlie and the Chocolate Factory* by Roald Dahl

---

*Spend **30 minutes** on this section.*

1 Which ingredients of a description does this text contain? Tick as many as you can identify.

Time of year ☐

Time of day ☐

Objects/People ☐

Movement ☐

Colours ☐

Sounds ☐

General landscape ☐

Textures ☐   [1]

2 Look at the first paragraph (lines 1–5). What is the name of the literary device used in this quotation?

'This is the <u>nerve</u> centre of the whole factory, <u>the heart</u> of the whole business!'

_____ [1]

3 Look at the first paragraph (lines 1–5). Give **one** word or phrase that suggests that the chocolate room could be dangerous.

_____ [1]

4 Look at the second paragraph (lines 6–7). The visitors are astonished by what they see. How do you know? Find **one** word which means astonishing.

_____ [1]

5 Look at the first paragraph (lines 1–5). What do we learn about Mr Wonka from the word 'insist' in this quotation?

'I insist upon my rooms being beautiful!'

_____ [1]

6 Why does the writer make the first paragraph nearly all speech by Mr Wonka?

_____ [2]

7 Look at the second paragraph (lines 6–7). Why does the writer use a dash after the word 'in'?

_____ [1]

8 Look at the second paragraph (lines 6–7). What does the word 'pushed' suggest in the following quotation?

Five children and nine grown-ups pushed their ways in.

_____ [1]

9 **a** Look at the third and fourth paragraphs (lines 8–12). Pick out **two** examples of the writer using adjectives to add detail.

  i _____

  ii _____

  [1]

  b Select **one** of the phrases and explain exactly what the adjective used means.

  Phrase A / B

  Meaning

  _____

  _____ [1]

  c Explain how this word helps you to imagine the scene that is being described.

  _____

  _____

  _____ [1]

10 Look at the fourth paragraph (lines 10–12). The writer uses two powerful verbs to describe the movement of the liquid chocolate water. Copy these out below.

  1 _____

  2 _____

  [1]

11 Look at the fourth paragraph (lines 10–12). Why is one long sentence used to describe the waterfall?

  _____ [1]

12 In the fifth paragraph (lines 13–20), the writer uses a number of descriptive techniques to describe the setting. Complete the table below, naming **two** of the techniques that the writer uses and giving an example from the text.

Technique	Example
	'suck-suck-sucking sound'
repetition	

  [2]

13 Look at the seventh paragraph (lines 24–30). Why did the writer use the following images when describing how much chocolate there was?

  'There's enough chocolate in there to fill every bathtub in the entire country! And all the swimming pools as well!'

  _____

  _____ [1]

14 Look at the seventh paragraph (lines 24–30). What do you think it shows about Mr Wonka when he says: '*And just look at my pipes!*'?

_____ [1]

15 Look at the seventh paragraph (lines 24–30). Mr Wonka uses quite formal English. Give **one** example.

_____ [1]

16 Look at lines 24–25. What does the word 'dancing' add to our impression of Mr Wonka's personality? Tick one answer.

A He likes to dance. ☐

B He has lots of energy. ☐

C He is excited. ☐ [1]

17 How is the chocolate carried to the rest of the factory?

_____ [1]

18 The chocolate room has been designed to look like a beautiful countryside valley.

a What are the connotations of a landscape like this?

_____

b Explain why the writer chose this landscape.

_____ [2]

19 a Overall, how would you sum up the atmosphere in the chocolate room? Tick one.

A Exciting ☐

B Thrilling ☐

C Happy ☐ [1]

b Write a paragraph explaining why you have chosen the word in part a, referring to two quotations from the text.

_____

_____

_____

_____ [1]

Section B: Writing

*Spend 45 minutes on this section in total. You may spend **15 minutes** planning your answer below.*

20 Imagine that you have arrived at a place you have never been to before. Write a description of your surroundings as you first take them in.

You could include:

- what you can see

- what you can hear and smell and, if appropriate, taste and touch

- how any people or animals are behaving

- how the place makes you feel.

Write your plan here.

Now write your description on a separate sheet of paper. [25]

Test 1: Non-fiction

Self-assessment for Section A: Reading

Focus	Marks available	My score
Language and vocabulary	**Subtotal: 5 marks**	
Understand literal meanings (Q4)	1	
Understand implicit meanings (Q5, Q6)	1, 2	
Explain effects of word choice or literary techniques (Q10)	1	
Text type, form, purpose and audience	**Subtotal: 8 marks**	
Recognise intended audience (Q8a)	1	
Identify the use of specific features (Q1)	2	
Explain the writer's use of specific features/techniques for a text type/form/purpose/audience (Q7, Q8b, Q11, Q13)	1, 1, 1, 2	
Understanding ideas and content	**Subtotal: 9 marks**	
Locate and retrieve information (Q2, Q3)	1, 1	
Take notes for a summary (Q16a)	3	
Summarise information (Q16b)	2	
Identify key issues or main points or themes (Q15a, 15b)	1, 1	
Structure, grammar and punctuation	**Subtotal: 3 marks**	
Recognise and/or comment on sentence/line structure (Q14)	1	
Comment on punctuation (Q9)	1	
Recognise and/or comment on grammatical features (Q12)	1	
TOTAL	**25**	

What I did well: _____

_____

_____

What I can improve: _____

_____

_____

Test 1: Non-fiction
Self-assessment for Section B: Writing

Focus	Checklist	✓	Marks available	My score
Ideas, planning and content	I made a useful plan or structure.		5	
	I ensured my answer was relevant to the task, its audience and purpose.			
	I included key features of the text/type form.			
	I made my voice or viewpoint clear.			
Language and vocabulary	I used a range of vocabulary.		3	
	I used vocabulary precisely.			
	I used words and phrases for effect.			
	I used language features or techniques for effect.			
Grammar and punctuation	I used a range of sentence types accurately.		7	
	I used different sentence types for clarity or emphasis.			
	I used punctuation accurately to make meaning clear.			
	I used formal or informal language appropriately.			
Paragraphing and structure	I used organisational features (where relevant).		7	
	I used paragraphs accurately and to help structure my text.			
	I used a range of connectives to link ideas.			
Spelling	I checked my spelling was accurate.		3	
TOTAL			**25**	

What I did well: _____

_____

_____

What I can improve: _____

_____

_____

Test 2: Fiction

Self-assessment for Section A: Reading

Focus	Marks available	My score
Language and vocabulary	**Subtotal: 8 marks**	
Explain literal meanings (Q3, Q4)	1, 1	
Understand implicit meanings (Q8)	1	
Identify linguistic or literary techniques (Q2, Q12)	1, 2	
Explain effects of word choice or literary techniques (Q9c, Q13)	1, 1	
Text type, form, purpose and audience	**Subtotal: 4 marks**	
Recognise/identify the use of specific features/techniques (Q1, Q9a)	1, 1	
Explain the writer's use of specific features/techniques for a text purpose/audience (Q9b, Q10)	1, 1	
Understanding ideas and content	**Subtotal: 8 marks**	
Locate and retrieve information (Q17)	1	
Recognise/identify mood, characterisation/relationships (Q5, Q16, Q19a)	1, 1, 1	
Comment on or explain how the writer creates mood, characters or relationships (Q14, Q18, Q19b)	1, 2, 1	
Structure, grammar and punctuation	**Subtotal: 5 marks**	
Comment on overall text structure (Q6)	2	
Comment on sentence structure (Q11)	1	
Comment on punctuation (Q7)	1	
Recognise grammatical features (Q15)	1	
TOTAL	**25**	

What I did well: _____

_____

_____

What I can improve: _____

_____

_____

Test 2: Fiction

Self-assessment for Section B: Writing

Focus	Checklist	✓	Marks available	My score
Ideas, planning and content	I made a useful plan or structure.		5	
	I ensured my answer was relevant to the task, purpose and form/genre.			
	I kept the reader interested.			
	I created a well-developed character.			
Language and vocabulary	I used a range of vocabulary.		3	
	I used vocabulary precisely.			
	I used words and phrases for effect.			
	I used literary techniques such as imagery.			
Grammar and punctuation	I used a range of sentence types accurately.		7	
	I used different sentence types for clarity or emphasis.			
	I used punctuation accurately.			
	I used punctuation to make meaning clear.			
Paragraphing and structure	My story or description has a logical structure.		7	
	I used a range of sentence openings.			
	I used paragraphs accurately to develop the narrative.			
	I used a range of connectives to link ideas.			
Spelling	I checked my spelling was accurate.		3	
TOTAL			**25**	

What I did well: _____

_____

_____

What I can improve: _____

_____

_____

Chapter 3: Understanding the differences between advice and persuasive texts

These tasks will help you to secure the following skills from Chapter 3 of the Student's Book:
- identify the features of advice and persuasive texts
- explore the use of positive and negative verbs, adjectives and phrases.

Read these two extracts from texts about safaris.

Text A

You may think safaris are ethical. Think again!

Picture the scene. A group of rich, impatient, sweaty tourists packed onto the back of a noisy truck, driving through the dusty Serengeti National Park. It is true they are holding cameras, and not hunting. But is this any better?

There is some evidence that humans have brought human diseases into the park which have been passed on to animals. And, are these animals really free? Or is this really just a giant zoo? Nowadays, some animals have become so tame, it is as if they have been trained so that smirking, self-satisfied tourists can get the perfect selfie.

5

Text B

How to choose the safari that is right for you.

Abroad or at home?

Before you book a safari on the other side of the world, consider what your own country can offer you. Although it can be good to explore new places abroad, you should research wildlife sanctuaries or parks closer to home. Many are cheap to visit or have some surprising species. Search for 'Local wildlife sanctuaries' on a search engine to see what is available.

5

Physical challenges

Some safaris are incredibly tiring and challenging. Are you fit enough? If not, consider doing some training before you go. For example, you could go on long walks or spend time camping in the fresh air. In addition, you might consider yoga or other stretching exercises.

10

1 Complete the table by ticking the relevant column for each feature.

Feature	Text A	Text B
1. Offers a single clear opinion.		
2. Creates strong, powerful images in the reader's mind.		
3. Uses subheadings for different information.		
4. Uses alliteration to make a point memorable.		
5. Mentions a problem, and then offers a solution.		
6. Uses modal verbs (like 'should') to suggest the solution.		
7. Uses rhetorical questions.		

2   Which of the texts is a persuasive text and which is an advice text?

Text A is _____.   Text B is _____.

The language used in each text matches the purpose of the writer. For example, a persuasive text might use very positive language about something the writer supports: 'The film is *magnificent*!'

3   In Text A, the writer uses several negative adjectives to describe tourists. Write **two** adjectives from paragraph one and **two** adjectives from paragraph two, used negatively.

Paragraph one: _____   _____

Paragraph two: _____   _____

Persuasive writing can tell us things directly ('The film is terrible!') or imply the same idea in a different way ('There are better ways to spend your evening, such as taking a bath in cold soup!').

4   Look at paragraph two in Text A. What do the adjectives imply about the tourists? Tick one answer.

  a   They are thankful to their guides for giving them the opportunity.   ☐

  b   They are very pleased with themselves for doing the safari.   ☐

  c   They are not enjoying the safari and wish it would end.   ☐

With writing to advise and writing to persuade, the reader is more likely to accept what is written if the writer seems knowledgeable.

5   Look at Text B. The writer uses language which shows that they are knowledgeable about local wildlife centres. Copy **two** phrases that show this.

Phrase 1 _____   Phrase 2 _____

6   In Text B, what suggestions does the writer make, if you are considering a safari which requires fitness?

The writer suggests that _____

_____

7   Do you agree with the writer of Text A? Write a paragraph giving your own opinion. Try to include at least one powerful positive or negative adjective and explain your viewpoint.

You could begin:

I strongly believe that _____

_____

_____

_____

Chapter 3: Making inferences and using quotations

These tasks will help you to secure the following skills from Chapter 3 of the Student's Book:

- use inference to explain the meaning of words and phrases
- use quotations effectively when explaining ideas about texts.

Read the following letter to a newspaper.

Dear Editor,

I am appalled to hear that our much-loved city centre zoo is to be closed. The zoo has provided countless hours of enjoyment to people of all ages for many years. It is a place which increases knowledge, ignites interest in the natural world, and creates the environmentalists of the future. As a child I spent many happy hours magnetised by the fierce eyes of the tiger and the stunning colours of the peacocks. I recall marvelling at the sheer size of the elephants. How much better it is to see these magical creatures in real life rather than in a book or on a screen. A recent survey revealed that over 65% of the local population are against closure. Shutting down the zoo will be like a death in the family. We need to stop it now!

5

10

Yours,

Rohan Kumar

To work out what a writer means or feels, look closely at specific words or phrases.

Sometimes, the meaning from these words is *explicit* or obvious. For example, if a writer has written, 'I hate zoos', the verb 'hate' tells the reader directly what the writer feels.

However, the writer might choose to *imply* what they mean. This is less obvious. For example, if the writer states, 'Zoos are a stain on humanity', you would need to work out what the connotations of 'stain' are (perhaps dirty, unclean or ruining something).

1 What is the writer implying by saying that he 'spent many happy hours magnetised' by the sight of the tiger, when there is no actual magnet here? Tick **one** of these implicit meanings.

   a He was forced to step away from fear of the tiger. ☐

   b He couldn't stop himself looking at the tiger in wonder. ☐

   c He wasted many hours near the tiger cage. ☐

When you explain the effect of a writer's language, you need to select examples from the text to support your ideas.

2 Underline **two** words in the following extract which suggest the writer found going to the zoo enchanting or miraculous.

> I recall marvelling at the sheer size of the elephants. How much better it is to see these magical creatures in real life rather than in a book or on a screen.

To explain the effects of these quotations, you will need to:
- write down the point or idea that the writer is expressing
- include the quotation that supports this idea in quotation marks ('…')
- explain their effect or meaning.

3 Complete this explanation using the words you selected from question 2 and adding your own inferences.

The writer uses the words '_____' and '_____' to explain his reaction to

animals during his childhood visits to the zoo. These words suggest _____, as if the visit

was like being in a dream or under a spell.

4 Now look at this extract from the text.

> The zoo has provided countless hours of enjoyment to people of all ages for many years. It is place which increases knowledge, ignites interest in the natural world, and creates the environmentalists of the future.

a Underline a phrase that relates to making visitors more curious about nature.

b Complete this paragraph.

The writer believes the zoo should remain open because it makes visitors _____

_____.

He says that a visit to such a place '_____'.

The word '_____' suggests that seeing nature up close can _____

_____.

5 Now read this letter from someone who supports the zoo's closure.

> While I was one of many children who enjoyed visiting the zoo when young, the sad truth is that the zoo has been totally neglected in recent years. The cages look rusty and need repainting, the information signs are faded and out of date and the animals themselves look bored and depressed. Let's end this farce, once and for all.
>
> Soraya N

Write a paragraph summing up Soraya's view, including at least one quotation from the text. Start:

Soraya believes that _____

_____.

_____.

_____.

_____.

_____.

_____.

Chapter 3: Structuring and developing ideas in advice texts

These tasks will help you to secure the following skills from Chapter 3 of the Student's Book:

- structure an advice text effectively
- use complex sentences in your writing to develop ideas.

Read the following extract from a travel blog written by an experienced traveller.

How to behave on safari in the Serengeti National Park

Going on safari is a once-in-a-lifetime experience. But it is important to be prepared and to act responsibly.

Respect the wildlife – it is wild, after all

Remember, you are not in a zoo nor are you at home with your pets. Often, there will be no barriers between you and the wildlife. Animals in the park are dangerous. For example, you may have only encountered elephants in films or in zoos. Although elephants can be gentle and approachable, they can also get easily spooked and charge. Make sure you are with an experienced local guide who knows when it is time to stay and watch, and when it is time to leave.   5

10

Wear suitable clothing and bring liquids

While you will spend most of your time in a truck, a safari can be tiring. So, take lots of water because you will be far from camp for most of the day. You should also wear comfortable clothing. You do not need to camouflage yourself with leopard-print designs, but neutral colours will help. Finally, you may think you are well-covered, but the sun can be very strong. For that reason, you must ensure you have a wide-brimmed hat.   15

Vocabulary

Serengeti National Park: a large, protected area in Northern Tanzania

---

When you write an advice text, you need to include its distinctive *features*.

1 Find and underline *at least one example* of each of the following features used in the text. Label each example with **a**, **b** or **c** next to it.

   a Imperative verbs telling you what you should do (for example, 'Go…!')

   b Modal verbs expressing obligation (for example, 'You *ought to* apologise to your friend.')

   c Modal verbs expressing possibility (for example, 'You *might/may* believe what she says.')

2 Now, write your own advice sentences.

   a Use a strong modal verb in a sentence about the need to use sunscreen on the safari.

      You _____.

   b Use a less strong modal verb in a sentence about the possibility of packing some warmer clothing for night-time.

      You _____.

Texts are deliberately structured and organised to help guide or direct the reader.

3   What phrase under the main heading makes readers want to read on?

_____

4   How does the use of subheadings help the reader? Write a brief explanation.

_____

_____

5   Advice texts often contain problems and solutions. Underline and label at least one problem identified by the writer in the text, then underline and label the solution.

6   Subordinating conjunctions can be used to link clauses. For example, the writer says:

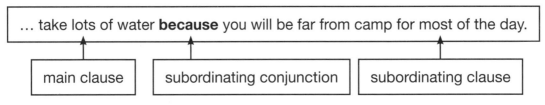

Copy **one** sentence from each of paragraphs two and three that starts with a subordinating conjunction to develop or explain an idea.

Paragraph two: _____

Paragraph three: _____

7   Using any of these subordinating conjunctions, complete the following complex sentences.

| Although   While   When   If |

a _____ you do not need expensive binoculars, they will be useful for spotting wildlife.

b _____ you are worried about something, ask your guide for advice.

8   Now, write two paragraphs to add to the advice text about safaris. Write about the importance of taking **two** of the following: a camera, guidebook or app, footwear, insect repellent.

Subheading 1:	_____
Text:	Remember You should
Subheading 2:	_____
Text:	Although You might

Chapter 4: Understanding mystery stories and their openings

These tasks will help you to secure the following skills from Chapter 4 of the Student's Book:
- identify the features and structures of mysterious or suspenseful stories
- identify the different ways story writers capture the reader's interest.

Mystery or suspense stories need to create drama and tension.

Read this story summary.

> Many years back, a young villager lives in a poor family. She helps by growing herbs to sell at a market. One day, a mysterious scroll with a map appears on her doorstep. It states: 'Follow the map to find your fortune.' She cannot decide what to do. She has heard that other young villagers have received similar messages and have left never to return. She decides to take the chance.   5
>
> In the night, she sets off. The map takes her deep into a wild forest. She quickly becomes lost. Frightened of wolves, she carves a bow and arrow. That night, as she dozes by a fire, wolves encircle her. They close in. Snarling, they force her back. But using her bow and arrows and then flaming branches, she drives them off just as dawn breaks. She is exhausted but alive.   10
>
> After resting, she continues. The map is complicated but she finally works out how to leave the forest. Ahead of her in a valley is a large mansion. At the gates, a servant lets her in, saying, 'My lord has been waiting for you.' In a huge hall, an elderly, sick-looking man sits on a throne. He tells her she has passed his test. All the other young villagers lost their way or were killed by wild animals. He tells her she will replace him when he   15
dies. He has no heirs and young blood is needed. He gives her a pouch of gold coins and tells her to return to her village. One day, she will be ruler.

A key feature of stories is the overall structure.

1 What does the reader learn about the character and her situation at the *beginning* of the story, before things change?

We learn that she _____

_____

2 What mysterious thing happens that changes her situation and gets the story moving?

The key change is when she _____

_____

3 What obstacles or problems does she face in the *middle part* of the story?

She faces a number of obstacles such as _____

_____

4 What is the most dramatic moment, when tension or excitement is at its highest?

The most dramatic moment is when _____

_____

After the tension falls away, the writer moves towards *resolution* (things being sorted out).

5 The *ending* of the story resolves the mystery from the beginning. What do we find out?

We learn that the quest was _____

and that _____

Here is one way the story could open.

Aya was just about to leave for the market when she saw it. A thin scroll with a simple red ribbon around it lay on the dusty floor. Her name was scratched on it in jagged ink. She never, ever received any letters. Nothing interesting ever happened to her. What could it be? She bent down quickly, and picked up the scroll, and then, with her heart racing and her dark, slim hands trembling, she fumbled with the blood-coloured ribbon and slowly unrolled the thin paper. She was about to read it when the door from the only other room in the tiny hut creaked open.   5

'Aya? You should have left by now. It's market day. You'll be late.' It was her mother. Aya scrunched the scroll up and stuffed it inside her shirt. Had her mother seen it? Her mother stared at her for a moment. Then, abruptly, she turned away, picking up a broom.   10

'Go on, then! Off you go!'

6 Story openings capture the reader's interest in many ways. Underline and label the following features in the text above:

A withholding information

B revealing selective information about the character's situation

C short, sharp sentences for dramatic action or thoughts

D questions to show the main character's uncertainty or excitement

E longer, multi-part sentences to build up atmosphere or develop description

7 Explain how the writer uses one of the techniques listed in question 6 to interest the reader. Include evidence for what you write.

_____

_____

_____

_____

_____

_____

_____

_____

Chapter 4: Exploring how writers create characters

These tasks will help you to secure the following skills from Chapter 4 of the Student's Book:

- identify and comment on the ways writers create characters
- empathise with characters.

The following extract is from a story called 'Fate'. We find out at the start that Mo Fei, the narrator, is paraplegic and lost the use of his legs several years earlier.

It was only an accident of one second's duration. To talk about it now is of little interest. It was a summer night, cloudy; the moon was pale, the stars few, and pedestrians were already very scarce. A night soil cart came by mingling the rich perfume of night soil with the sweet scent of evening dew – a rare odour. I was riding my bike home, so happy that I had naturally begun whistling a tune. I was whistling the famous   5
pedlar's **aria** from ***The Pedlar and the Maiden***. I had just been to the opera. I really belicved my luck was pretty good. I was soon to go abroad to study; my thoughts were concentrated on that side, of course; the world is very large. My wallet was already crammed full with my passport, visa, plane ticket, and a wad of related documents – the fruits of one year and eleven months of difficult struggle. This wallet was firmly   10
attached to my belt; unless somebody ripped off my trousers, it would be quite impossible to lose it. May the designer of this wallet be richly rewarded in this life and the next – that's what I was thinking at the time. The temperature fell gradually and a slightly cool breeze began to blow. In the buildings along the road someone was cursing loudly while another was softly playing a **nocturne** by **Chopin**. The out-of-town   15
street vendors were spreading their baggage out in the shadows, yawning broadly, making a racket as loud as an ancient nightwatchman's.

An ordinary summer's night.

From 'Fate' by Shi Tie-sheng

Vocabulary

aria: a long solo song in an opera

The Pedlar and the Maiden: a Chinese myth and opera

nocturne: piece of music inspired by night-time

Chopin: famous Polish pianist and composer

Writers make the reader interested in characters in a range of ways. The first is perspective.

1 a Is this story told in the first person (using 'I') or third person (using 'he', 'she' or 'they')?

_____

b How does this help you to understand the perspective of the main character?

_____

Equally important is *what* writers tell us about characters.

2 Look at line 1 and at the introductory text about the story. What has happened to Mo Fei that makes him an unusual character?

We find out that _____

Writers also tell us about their character's feelings.

3 Look at lines 4–8. What does the writer tell us about Mo Fei's state of mind that evening?

Mo Fei felt _____ because _____

_____

4 In what way does the writer withhold information to keep us interested?

Although the narrator says, 'It was only an accident of one second's duration', we are not yet told

_____

Characters can have a range of emotions and behave in different ways at different times.

5 Underline or highlight evidence in the text for the following statements. Label each one A, B or C.

A Mo Fei is in good spirits at this time.

B Mo Fei has a good sense of humour.

C Mo Fei is a hard worker.

6 Why does the reader feel empathy for Mo Fei? Think about the title of the story and about what you know is about to happen to Mo Fei.

Write a paragraph including some of the quotations you underlined or highlighted in question 5.

During the extract, we find out that Mo Fei is in very good spirits as he states that _____

_____

We also know that life hasn't been easy because _____

_____

The title of the story is 'Fate'. This means _____

_____

_____

It suggests that whatever you do, you can't avoid _____

This creates empathy for Mo Fei because _____

_____

_____

Chapter 4: Structuring story openings and introducing characters

Securing

These tasks will help you to secure the following skills from Chapter 4 of the Student's Book:

- generate ideas for a suspense story
- plan and structure an opening featuring a character.

1 Add notes to the spider diagram to plan a story based around the title 'The abandoned house'.

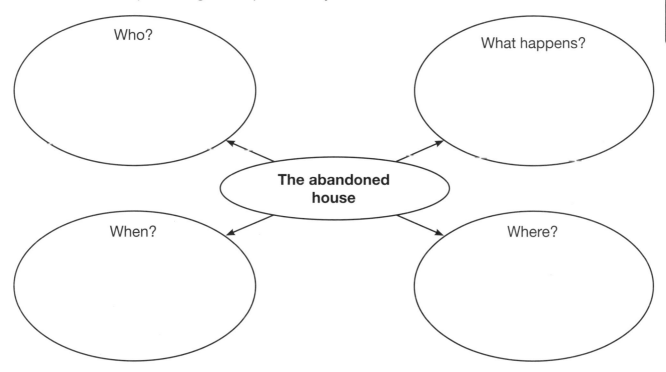

2 Now, think more about your plot.

Use the grid below to make more detailed notes about the story that you are planning.

Part of story	Your notes
Opening Where and when does it begin? Who and what is revealed – or *not* revealed? How does the situation change or develop?	
Middle What obstacles, problems or challenges does the main character face? What is the main dramatic or exciting moment?	
Ending How are the problems or challenges resolved? What mysteries are tied up or revealed?	

Now think more about your main character or *protagonist*.

Consider:

- physical details: your character's height, build, face, hair
- background: their family, friends, interests
- character or behaviour: Are they confident or shy? Sporty? Hard-working?
- relationships: how they get on with family, friends, others
- why a reader might empathise with them. For example, what difficulties they have faced or are facing.

3 Write some background notes describing your main character.

My character is called _____

He/she/they is/are _____

_____

_____

_____

_____

_____

_____

_____

4 You are now going to write the opening of your story, featuring your main character. Decide whether to write in the first or third person.

- *Show* rather than tell information about your character. For example, in 'Fate', Mo Fei is cycling home 'whistling a tune'. This shows us he is happy.

- Use well-chosen verbs, adjectives and adverbs to reveal how your character or others behave. For example, 'I *hid shyly* in my attic room, *burying* my head in my *favourite* graphic novel.'

- Use well-chosen dialogue and punctuation to make your opening come to life.

You could use one of these prompts.

Prompt 1: *He longed to get away from his argumentative, crowded family. As he sat by his bedroom window, the abandoned house across the street seemed to call out to him...*

Prompt 2: *I couldn't believe she was making me do this. Here we stood, in front of the broken windows...*

Prompt 3: *'Hey, Captain! Shall we search that house?' One of my men stood beside me, fear etched on his face...*

Write your story opening on a separate sheet of paper.

Test 3: NON-FICTION

This test is 90 minutes long (including 30 minutes of reading and planning time).

Section A: Reading

Spend 45 minutes on this section.

*Before you answer the test questions, spend **15 minutes** reading and making notes.*

Read this newspaper article which relates to a dangerous natural occurrence.

As you are reading, note down your answers to the big five questions.

- What is the purpose of this text?
- What is the article about?
- Where are the events or issues taking place?
- Who do you think this article is for?
- Why has the writer written this text?

(These notes are to help you prepare for the test. They will not be given marks.)

How to stay safe from avalanches when skiing – everything you need to know

Here are Henry Schniewind's, of Henry's Avalanche Talks (HAT), top tips on how to survive dangerous snow situations and stay safe in the mountains.

How to be prepared for an avalanche

1. Know what the danger ratings mean

Familiarise yourself with the five international avalanche danger levels: 1 is low risk of avalanches, 2 is moderate, 3 is considerable, 4 is high and 5 is extreme.

5

---

2. Check the forecast

Read the official avalanche forecast bulletin for your area the evening before you head out – this will tell you the altitude and slope aspects where the risk is greatest. This will be available in the resort.

3. Stick with like-minded riders

Travel with people who have a similar approach to having fun and being safe **off-piste**. Keep your group size to between three and five people – if there are only two of you and one gets caught, the other one will be alone, needing to both rescue you and to fetch help. If there are more than five of you, the group can become fragmented and the safety risks increase.

4. Carry all the equipment you need

If you're going off-piste skiing in winter, have all of the essentials with you – avalanche **transceiver**, **probe** and shovel – to get your friends out from under the snow in 15 minutes or less. After 15 minutes buried under snow, the chance of survival decreases rapidly.

5. Train with the safety equipment

Do a two- or three-hour practical session on how to use your safety equipment and refresh yourself each year. Know how your equipment works and make sure the others do as well – you are relying on them to rescue you.

6. Save the key phone numbers

You should have all the phone numbers for local rescue services on your phone.

7. Plan your routes

Have a good idea of the area and routes you'll be skiing (using maps, guide books and your personal experience) or hiking so you don't end up stuck on a cliff. Be alert to danger signs as you go. It is all too easy to let passion and enthusiasm blind you to risk.

8. Learn about slope angles

Know how to identify slopes of 30 degrees or more – this is where the majority of avalanches occur.

9. Talk to local professionals

People like the ski patrol (**piste** patrol) and mountain guides are a good source of insider information on the area.

From *The Telegraph*, 17 March 2023

10

15

20

25

30

35

Vocabulary

off-piste: away from designated ski-runs

transceiver: device which emits a signal from under snow

probe: stick for locating buried people

piste: a ski-run of compacted snow (created for skiers)

Spend 30 minutes on this section.

1 List **four** further features that suggest that this is an advice text.

1 Use of imperative verbs ('**Plan** your routes', '**Check** the forecast')

2 _____

3 _____

4 _____

5 _____ [2]

2 How many international danger levels are there?

_____ [1]

3 Look at lines 8–9. Which word meaning 'weather prediction' does the writer use?

_____ [1]

4 Look at lines 18–20. Which word means 'most important items'?

_____ [1]

5 Look at the following sentence from the text. Which very short connective word introduces a possible problem?

If there are only two of you and one gets caught, the other one will be alone, needing to both rescue you and to fetch help.

_____ [1]

6 Look at line 9. Which five-word phrase means 'where the dangers are the worst'?

_____ [1]

7 Look at lines 13–16. Which word suggests that groups can end up being divided if there are too many people in them?

_____ [1]

8 a What audience is this text written for? Tick **one** box.

- Young children ☐
- Experienced ski guides ☐
- Keen skiers ☐
- People who don't like skiing ☐ [1]

b Why do you think that?

_____

_____

_____ [1]

9 a What do you think is the main message about skiing off-piste, based on this article? Tick **one** answer.

A It should be avoided. ☐

B It's easy to do. ☐

C It's fun but can be dangerous. ☐

D It's lonely. ☐ [1]

b Explain why you think this.

_____

_____ [1]

10 Why does the writer use short subheadings throughout the article?

_____ [1]

11 Look at lines 34–35. What is the purpose of the dash in the sentence?

Know how to identify slopes of 30 degrees or more – this is where the majority of avalanches occur.

_____ [1]

12 a Look at line 27. Underline the modal verb used in this sentence.

You should have all the phone numbers for local rescue services on your phone. [1]

b What meaning does the modal verb in part **a** add to the sentence? Tick **one** answer.

A This is something you could do if you like. ☐

B This is something you ought to do. ☐

C This is something you ought not to do. ☐

D This is something you are not able to do. ☐ [1]

13 Look at lines 29–32. Underline the connecting word which gives the consequence of not knowing the area.

Have a good idea of the area and routes you'll be skiing (using maps, guide books and your personal experience) or hiking so you don't end up stuck on a cliff. Be alert to danger signs as you go. It is all too easy to let passion and enthusiasm blind you to risk. [1]

14 What tense is used in the following sentence?

People like the ski patrol (piste patrol) and mountain guides are a good source of insider information on the area.

_____ [1]

15 What problems and solutions are mentioned in sections 3 and 4?

Section 3

The possible problem is _____

The suggested solution is _____

Section 4

The possible problem is _____

The suggested solution is _____ [2]

16 A skier reading this article before a holiday decides to make their own notes. Complete their table of notes below.

What skiers should do...	Notes
...in general preparation or training	
...just before skiing (e.g. the day before or on the day)	
...while they are skiing	

[3]

17 Using the information in the notes above, write a summary of up to 50 words about what you should do when you go skiing.

_____

_____

_____

_____ [2]

Section B: Writing

*Spend 45 minutes on this section. You may spend **15 minutes** planning your answer below.*

18 Write an advice article for a website aimed at people who like mountain biking. (Mountain biking refers to any biking activity when someone goes off normal roads and cycles on rough paths or terrain.)

You should consider:

- what equipment they might need to keep them safe

- how they can prepare in advance in other ways

- how they might cope with any problems.

Write your plan here.

Now write your advice article on a separate sheet of paper.

[25]

Test 4: FICTION

This test is 90 minutes long (including 30 minutes of reading and planning time).

Section A: Reading

Spend 45 minutes on this section.

*Before you answer the test questions, spend **15 minutes** reading the text and making notes.*

Read the text extract.

As you are reading, note down your answers to the big five questions.

- Who is the extract about?
- What is happening in the extract?
- When are the events happening: now, in the past or in the future?
- Where do the events take place?
- Why has the writer written this text?

(These notes are to help you prepare for the test. They will not be given marks.)

An avalanche

Somewhere way up high, he heard a sound, as if something deep inside the mountain were splitting with a sigh. Then he heard a deep, swelling rumble and a moment later the ground beneath his feet began to tremble. Suddenly he was cold. Within seconds the rumbling had increased to a high, piercing note. Egger stood stock-still and heard the mountain start to sing. Then he saw something big and black hurtle silently past   5
about twenty metres away and before he had even grasped that it was a tree trunk he began to run. He ran back through the deep snow towards the house, calling to **Marie**, but an instant later something seized him and lifted him up. He felt himself being carried away and the last thing he saw before a dark wave engulfed him was his legs, sticking up above him into the sky as if disconnected from the rest of his body.   10

When Egger came to, the clouds had disappeared and in the night sky the moon was a radiant white. All around the mountains soared up in its light; their icy crests looked as if they had been punched from a sheet of metal, their sharpness and clarity seeming to cut into the sky. Egger was lying on his back at an angle. He could move his head and arms, but his legs were buried up to the hips in snow. He began to dig. Using   15
both hands he shovelled and scratched his legs out of the snow and when he had freed them he saw them lying there, stunned, as cold and alien as two planks of wood. He pounded his thighs with his fists. 'Don't abandon me now,' he said, and finally gave a hoarse laugh as pain shot into them along with the blood. He tried to stand, but immediately buckled again. […] 'Come on, up you get!' he said to himself, and when he   20
tried again he managed it, and stood. The landscape had changed. The avalanche had buried trees and rocks beneath it and levelled the ground. The deep snow lay like a vast blanket in the moonlight. He tried to get his bearings from the mountains. As far as he could tell, he was about three hundred metres below his cabin, which must be up there behind the mound of piled-up snow. He set off.   25

From *A Whole Life* by Robert Seethaler

Vocabulary

Marie: Egger's wife

Spend 30 minutes on this section.

1   Which features of a suspense story does this text contain? Write as many as you can think of. For example:

Exciting or tense action or events

_____

_____

_____

_____

_____

_____

_____ [1]

2   Look at lines 1–2. What is the first thing that Egger notices at the start of the story?

_____ [1]

3   Look at the first paragraph. Give **two** phrases that suggest the mountain is making musical sounds.

Phrase 1 _____

Phrase 2 _____ [2]

4   Look at lines 5–7. What verb describes how the tree moves past at very high speed?

_____ [1]

5   Look at line 9. What is the writer suggesting happened to Egger when it says 'a dark wave engulfed him'?

_____ [1]

6   Why does the writer choose to start a new a paragraph after the end of paragraph one?

_____ [1]

7   Look at lines 12–14. The writer uses **two** similes to describe the tops of the mountains. What similes does he use?

Simile 1 _____

Simile 2 _____ [2]

8   Explain how the similes in question 7 help us to imagine the scene.

_____ [1]

9 Underline the **two** verbs meaning 'dug' and 'scraped' in the following sentence from lines 15–17 of the story.

Using both hands he shovelled and scratched his legs out of the snow and when he had freed them he saw them lying there, stunned, as cold and alien as two planks of wood. [1]

10 What does the following underlined simile suggest about Egger's feelings about his legs?

he saw them lying there, stunned, <u>as cold and alien as two planks of wood</u>.

_____ [1]

11 Look at line 18. What does the verb 'pounded' mean in the following sentence?

He pounded his thighs with his fists.

_____ [1]

12 Look at line 19. Why does Egger 'laugh' when 'pain' shoots through his legs?

_____ [1]

13 a Look at line 20. What does the direct speech 'Come on, up you get!' suggest about Egger's character? Tick **one** answer.

    A He likes talking to himself. ☐

    B He is determined to overcome his problems. ☐

    C He is lonely. ☐

    D He is worried about Marie. ☐ [1]

b Why? Explain your choice.

_____ [1]

c What does the use of an exclamation mark tell us about how Egger speaks?

_____ [1]

14 Look at lines 22–23. What does the simile 'like a vast blanket' tell the reader about the snow?

_____ [1]

15 In the first paragraph, how does the writer build up the tension? Complete this table.

Technique	Example
Withholding information	
	'Suddenly he was cold.'
Long compound or complex sentence which gives lots of detail about what happens to Egger	

[3]

16 The extract describes Egger's experiences in stages. Put these parts of his story in the correct order by adding numbers 1 (first in the story) to 5 (last) to each letter.

A He sets off to find his cabin.

B He hears a sound in the mountains but doesn't know what it is.

C He wakes up.

D He is knocked unconscious by the avalanche.

E He manages to dig himself out of the snow.

_____ [2]

17 a Overall, how would you sum up the atmosphere of the story so far? Tick **one** answer.

    A Exciting

    B Tense

    C Peaceful [1]

    b Explain why, using one sentence and including at least one quotation from the text.

_____

_____

_____

_____ [1]

Section B: Writing

*Spend 45 minutes on this section. You may spend **15 minutes** planning your answer below.*

18 Write part of a story in which someone tries to rescue someone or something precious. This could be a friend, relative or animal, for example.

You should consider:

- what caused the precious person/animal to become trapped

- when and where it is found

- what needs to be done to rescue it

- how you can make the story as tense and dramatic as possible.

Write your plan here.

Now write your story on a separate sheet of paper. [25]

Test 3: Non-fiction

Self-assessment for Section A: Reading

Focus	Marks available	My score
Language and vocabulary	**Subtotal: 3 marks**	
Understand literal meanings (Q3, Q4)	1, 1	
Understand implicit meanings (Q6)	1	
Text type, form, purpose and audience	**Subtotal: 7 marks**	
Identify the writer's purpose/intended audience (Q8a)	1	
Identify the use of specific features/techniques (Q14, Q15)	1, 2	
Explain the writer's use of specific features/techniques for a text type/purpose/audience (Q1, Q8b)	2, 1	
Understanding ideas and content	**Subtotal: 9 marks**	
Locate and retrieve information (Q2, Q7)	1, 1	
Take notes for a summary (Q16)	3	
Summarise information (Q17)	2	
Recognise/identify key issues or main points or themes (Q9a, Q9b)	1, 1	
Structure, grammar and punctuation	**Subtotal: 6 marks**	
Recognise sentence/line structure (Q5, Q13)	1, 1	
Comment on punctuation (Q11)	1	
Recognise and/or comment on presentational or organisational features (Q10)	1	
Comment on grammatical features (Q12a, Q12b)	1, 1	
TOTAL	**25**	

What I did well: _____

_____

_____

What I can improve: _____

_____

_____

Test 3: Non-fiction

Self-assessment for Section B: Writing

Focus	Checklist	✓	Marks available	My score
Ideas, planning and content	I made a useful plan or structure.		5	
	I ensured my answer was relevant to the task, its audience and purpose.			
	I included key features of the text type/form.			
	I made my voice or viewpoint clear.			
Language and vocabulary	I used a range of vocabulary.		3	
	I used vocabulary precisely.			
	I used words and phrases for effect.			
	I used other language features or techniques for effect (like imperative verbs).			
Grammar and punctuation	I used a range of sentence types accurately.		7	
	I used different sentence types for clarity or emphasis.			
	I used punctuation accurately.			
	I used punctuation to make meaning clear.			
	I used formal or informal language appropriately.			
Paragraphing and structure	I used organisational features (where relevant).		7	
	I used paragraphs accurately and to help structure my text.			
	I used a range of connectives to link ideas.			
Spelling	I checked my spelling was accurate.		3	
TOTAL			**25**	

What I did well: _____

_____

_____

What I can improve: _____

_____

_____

Test 4: Fiction

Self-assessment for Section A: Reading

Focus	Marks available	My score
Language and vocabulary	**Subtotal: 8 marks**	
Understand literal meanings (Q4, Q11)	1, 1	
Understand implicit meanings (Q3)	2	
Explain implicit meanings (Q5)	1	
Recognise linguistic or literary techniques (Q7)	2	
Explain effects of word choice/linguistic, literary or dramatic techniques (Q8)	1	
Text type, form, purpose and audience	**Subtotal: 2 marks**	
Identify the use of specific features/techniques (Q1)	1	
Explain the writer's use of specific features/techniques for a text type/form/purpose/audience (Q10)	1	
Understanding ideas and content	**Subtotal: 9 marks**	
Locate and retrieve information (Q2)	1	
Identify key issues or main points or themes (Q16)	2	
Identify mood, characterisation/relationships (Q12, Q17a)	1, 1	
Comment on or explain how the writer creates mood, characters or relationships (Q13a, Q13b, Q14, Q17b)	1, 1, 1, 1	
Structure, grammar and punctuation	**Subtotal: 4 marks**	
Comment on overall text structure (Q6)	1	
Recognise paragraph/scene/stanza structure (Q15)	3	
Recognise sentence/line structure (Q9)	1	
Comment on punctuation (Q13c)	1	
TOTAL	**25**	

What I did well: _____

_____

_____

What I can improve: _____

_____

_____

Test 4: Fiction

Self-assessment for Section B: Writing

Focus	Checklist	✓	Marks available	My score
Ideas, planning and content	I made a useful plan or structure.		5	
	I ensured my answer was relevant to the task, purpose and form/genre.			
	I kept the reader interested.			
	I created a well-developed character.			
Language and vocabulary	I used a range of vocabulary.		3	
	I used vocabulary precisely.			
	I used words and phrases for effect.			
	I used literary techniques, such as imagery.			
Grammar and punctuation	I used a range of sentence types accurately.		7	
	I used different sentence types for clarity or emphasis.			
	I used punctuation accurately.			
	I used punctuation to make meaning clear.			
Paragraphing and structure	My story or description has a logical structure.		7	
	I used a range of sentence openings.			
	I used paragraphs accurately to develop the narrative.			
	I used a range of connectives to link ideas.			
Spelling	I checked my spelling was accurate.		3	
TOTAL			**25**	

What I did well: _____

_____

_____

What I can improve: _____

_____

_____

These tasks will help you to secure the following skills from Chapter 5 of the Student's Book:
- explore the conventions and presentation of ideas in playscripts
- develop your own ideas for plays.

Playscripts look very different from stories in the way they are set out on the page. Look at this very short extract from a story and how it might look as a playscript.

Story	Play
She was about to read it when the door from the only other room in the tiny hut creaked open.	AYA *is by the door in her parents' hut, holding the scroll. Suddenly, she hears a noise.*
'Aya? You should have left by now. It's market day. You'll be late.' It was her mother.	MOTHER: (*entering*) Aya? You should have left by now. It's market day. You'll be late.
Aya scrunched the scroll up and stuffed it inside her shirt. Had her mother seen it? Her mother stared at her for a moment. Then, abruptly, she turned away, picking up a broom.	AYA *scrunches up the scroll, nervously stuffs it inside her shirt.*
	MOTHER *stares at her, then picks up a broom.*
'Go on, then! Off you go!'	MOTHER: Go on, then! Off you go!

1 What similarities do you notice between the two texts?

    They are similar because they both _____

    _____

2 What differences do you notice in the way the playscript presents the story?

    a How does the text look on the page? For example, where do the speakers' names go?

    _____

    _____

    b What language is used? For example, which tense?

    _____

    _____

    c How are actions and thoughts shown?

    _____

    _____

3 Now, write a list of rules or conventions which someone writing a play should follow. You could start:

    - Details about where the action takes place must be given in the notes about staging or set design.

    - Names of speaking characters must be written on the _____

    - _____

- _____

- _____

Plays share some similarities with short stories. The main character often faces obstacles or challenges and has to overcome them to get what they want. But everything needs to either be shown on stage through action or through what people say.

4 You are going to write the opening scene of a play called *The New Kid*. It will be about a new student who starts at a school.

a Begin by making notes.

What happens in the play? Does the new kid make friends easily? Or make enemies? Do they change or surprise others?	
Who is involved? Apart from the new kid, who are the main speaking characters?	
When does it take place? Is it set in the present day, the past – or perhaps the future?	
Where does it take place? Will the opening scene be set in the classroom or perhaps somewhere else, such as the playground, canteen or local park? Remember, you will need to show these locations on stage.	
Any other details	

b Write your first scene, using the conventions of a play layout.

You could begin:

SCENE 1: *Morning. Just before registration. A modern classroom with rows of tables. A group of three students – KATYA, LEE and RAJ – are sitting at a table laughing at a video on their phones. Enter JUNE, with short, spiky hair. She has bright red glasses.*

JUNE: *(nervously)* Umm. Is this… er… Class 8G?

LEE: *(looking up)* Yep. Sure is.

JUNE: _____

_____

_____

_____

_____

_____

Chapter 5: Exploring and using the structure and language of reviews

These tasks will help you to secure the following skills from Chapter 5 of the Student's Book:
- explore the key structural features and content of reviews
- use effective language to write a review.

Read this extract from a review of a play called *Moon on a Rainbow Shawl*.

Moon on a Rainbow Shawl (by Errol John)

Review by Kate Kellaway

It is marvellous to report that, 55 years on, this play, in its original version, holds its own and seems fresh as the day it was written. It is set in a dirt-poor Trinidadian yard with blue verandah, scruffy greenery and rickety stairs (designer: Soutra Gilmour). And we get to know the people living in it as if we were their neighbours. Thanks to an intimately reconstituted **Cottesloe** (audiences on both sides of the stage), we are. 5

A mother is at the heart of the drama. Sophia Adams, beautifully played by Martina Laird, is far more than the stereotypical West Indian **matriarch** no one dares to cross – although she has perfected the art of the straight look.

From *The Guardian*, 18 March 2012

Vocabulary

Cottesloe: one of the stages at the National Theatre, London

matriarch: female head of a family

Reviews need to contain some key information. Usually, this includes:

- information about the title of the play or film and the writer and/or director's name
- a summary of the plot, including the main characters, with comments on how effective it is
- comments and information on the staging, design or cinematography
- comments and information on the acting and/or directing.

These details should make clear what the overall reviewer's viewpoint is.

1 Look again at the four bullet points above. Using a different colour for each point, underline or highlight the review to identify where each one has been covered.

2 What isn't really covered yet in any detail?

_____

3 a What do you notice about the tense used to describe the story, setting and acting?

_____

b Why do you think a review is generally written in this way?

_____

4 The writer uses **three** words or phrases in the sentence below to give a positive view of the play as a whole. Underline them.

> It is marvellous to report that, 55 years on, this play, in its original version, holds its own and seems fresh as the day it was written.

5 The reviewer is also very positive about the staging in the theatre (the Cottesloe).

> And we get to know the people living in it as if we were their neighbours. Thanks to an intimately reconstituted **Cottesloe** (audiences on both sides of the stage), we are.

Complete this paragraph.

By saying that we watch the characters on stage 'as if we were their neighbours', it is suggesting that the

audience are _____

So, the overall effect when watching must be _____

_____

_____

6 Now, read this extract from another review.

   a Underline the negative words or phrases used.

   b Circle the verbs in the past tense.

> Unfortunately, this tired version of *Romeo and Juliet* was not worth seeing. There was dull, old-fashioned staging and the actor playing Romeo was unconvincing. He had a faint voice and a weak presence on stage.

7 Now, rewrite the review with more positive language and in the present tense. Use some of the words or phrases from the box.

fresh	excitingly	modern	powerful	believable
energetic	strong	magnetic	vibrant	up-to-date
lively	vivid	captivating	fortunately	refreshingly

_____

_____

_____

_____

_____

_____

Securing

These tasks will help you to secure the following skills from Chapter 6 of the Student's Book:
- analyse a poem's form and structure
- explain the effect of particular words and phrases.

Read the following poem about a fish by American poet Amy Lowell.

As you read:
- underline any powerful or vivid words, phrases or lines
- highlight any patterns – repeated words or sounds, rhyme or rhythm
- add questions or comments alongside anything you find difficult or curious
- add notes about how the poem is set out on the page.

The Pike

In the brown water,
Thick and silver-sheened in the sunshine,
Liquid and cool in the shade of the reeds,
A pike dozed.
Lost among the shadows of stems   5
He lay unnoticed.
Suddenly he flicked his tail,
And a green-and-copper brightness
Ran under the water.

Out from under the reeds   10
Came the olive-green light,
And orange flashed up
Through the sun-thickened water.
So the fish passed across the pool,
Green and copper,   15
A darkness and a gleam,
And the blurred reflections of the willows on the opposite bank
Received it.

                                                  By Amy Lowell

---

Understanding a poem's form and structure can help explore its meaning and impact.

1 Draw lines to link the line numbers to the summaries of parts of the poem.

Lines	What the set of lines is about
1–6	The colours of the light as it rises in the water
7–9	A pike asleep under the water
10–13	The pike moves across the pool, creating light and darkness in reflections of trees
14–18	The pike's sudden movement and what could be seen underwater

The poem describes in detail a simple thing – a fish moving and all the colours and light effects on the water around it.

2 Why do you think the poet delays mentioning the pike until line 4? (Think about what it would be like if you were someone watching the pool.)

I think not mentioning the pike at first creates _____

3 Read the poem again, aloud, thinking about how it is paced, including:

• how the lines are separated and whether they make you read it quickly or slowly

• whether there are moments where it speeds up or slows down.

I think overall the poem is meant to be read _____

4 How does the poem's pace, and the way it changes at particular points, match the meaning?

I think the poem starts with a long sentence broken up into four lines to make us read it slowly, as this

matches the _____

Another way of exploring the poem's impact is to look at word groupings or 'semantic fields'.

5 Find words or phrases in the poem which describe the following.

light and darkness	
colour and texture	
natural features, such as trees and plants	

Now, you can begin to explore the impact of individual words or phrases and any associations that they bring to mind.

For example:

In the brown water,   ── Muddy, unclear?

Thick and silver-sheened in the sunshine,   ── Texture is solid, strong, pleasant!

Liquid and cool in the shade of the reeds,

6 Add annotations to the lines above for the phrase 'silver-sheened'.

7 Now complete the following paragraph. Add quotations from the lines above.

The poet initially describes the water and the pike in a not particularly pleasant way. She describes how it is

'_____' and the pike is '_____', which conveys how _____

_____.

However, she then describes the pike as '_____', which suggests it has _____

_____, which looks _____.

Chapter 6: Exploring sounds and themes in poetry

These tasks will help you to secure the following skills from Chapter 6 of the Student's Book:
- identify sound techniques used by poets
- recognise and explain themes in poems.

Read the following poem about buffaloes, which used to exist in huge numbers in the USA.

As you read, underline and highlight key words, phrases and lines, adding your own notes and queries.

The Flower-fed Buffaloes

The flower-fed buffaloes of the spring
In the days of long ago,
Ranged where the **locomotives** sing
And the **prairie** flowers lie low:--
The tossing, blooming, perfumed grass   5
Is swept away by the wheat,
Wheels and wheels and wheels spin by
In the spring that still is sweet.
But the flower-fed buffaloes of the spring
Left us long ago.   10
They **gore** no more, they bellow no more,
They trundle around the hills no more:--
With the **Blackfeet**, lying low,
With the **Pawnees**, lying low,
Lying low.   15

By Vachel Lindsay

Vocabulary

locomotives: trains

prairie: flat grasslands in North America

gore: wound with horns or tusks

Blackfeet and **Pawnees:** names of Native American tribes

Sound can influence a poem's meaning, whether this is through rhythm, rhyme, repetition or the emphasis put on particular words or phrases. First, you need to identify the techniques the poet uses.

1 Complete this table, adding at least one example in each row.

Sound technique	Example/s	Line/s
rhyme		
emphatic rhythm	'Wheels and wheels and wheels spin by'	
repetition (of words or phrases)		
alliteration (repeated sounds at start of words, e.g. '**S**ilvery, **s**lim **s**nake')		
anything else you notice		

Spotting these techniques is useful – but what is their impact? One student said this: *Repeating the word 'wheels' three times emphasises the huge, never-ending number of trains which now dominate the fields where the buffalo once roamed.*

2 Why do you think the poet repeats the phrases 'long ago' and 'no more' when talking about the buffaloes?

_____

3 Look at the example in the table of emphatic or strong rhythm. How does this add to the impact of the machines that have led to the buffaloes disappearing?

_____

The poet conveys his themes and ideas through sound and form, but also language.

4 Read line 5: 'The tossing, blooming, perfumed grass'.

What impression does the poet give of the grass that used to grow in the time of the buffaloes?

The verb 'tossing' suggests continual movement, like dancing. 'Blooming' means _____,

which creates a picture of _____,

while 'perfumed' conveys _____

5 What does line 6, 'Is swept away by the wheat', suggest about farming?

'Swept away' means _____, so this suggests that he feels

_____

One of the repetitions you probably noticed was 'lie low' and 'lying low'. This can have two meanings: literally, to lie down close to the ground but also to keep out of sight or to hide.

6 What do you think is the significance of ending with the repeated phrase 'lying low' about the Native American tribes? Why might they be hiding? Who from?

_____

_____

7 What is the main idea or theme of the poem? Write a paragraph explaining your ideas.

The core theme or idea in this poem is that trains and farming have _____

_____

_____

8 Now, think about how the poet conveys these ideas to the reader by using sound and other techniques.

The poet emphasises how this happened in the past, and how the buffalo and wild land can't be brought back

by repeating phrases such as _____

The flowers that used to grow are described as _____

This suggests that they _____

The poet also uses repetition to stress the impact of the trains and farm machines, for example when

_____

_____

Test 5: NON-FICTION

This test is 90 minutes long (including 30 minutes of reading and planning time).

Section A: Reading

*Before you answer the test questions, spend **15 minutes** reading and making notes.*

Read this article about a film.

As you are reading, note down answers to the big five questions.

- What is the purpose of this text?
- What is the article about?
- Where and when do the events of the film take place?
- Who do you think this article is for?
- Why has the writer written this text?

(These notes are for your preparation for the test. They will not be given marks.)

The Film that Makes me Cry – *Up*

The somewhat unexpected hero of this 2009 Pixar classic is Carl Fredricksen, a balloon salesman in his late 70s who lives alone after the death of his wife Ellie. The animation starts further back in time, however, with Ellie and Carl meeting as wide-eyed, button-nosed children dreaming of exploration as they soar across the wilderness of their imaginary worlds in matching **aviator** goggles. 5

In quick succession, the two grow up, fall in love, get married and build a home together. But time presses urgently on, and soon we see Ellie on her deathbed handing Carl her well-loved book of adventures and telling him it's time for one of his own. Some films may try to tease out a tear at some point along the way and never quite achieve it; *Up* has you with this opening sequence and doesn't let you go. 10

Yet, magically, despite heart-wrenchingly understated scenes like Ellie's death, *Up* is always one step ahead, making you laugh out loud just when you least expect it. Carl's totally non-action-packed trip from the top to the bottom of his house via a stairlift is the perfect example – but perhaps you have to see that one to appreciate it. 15

Up is a film about getting old, about regret and about realising that life is messy and out of control, as much as you might try to make it otherwise. But it's also a film about love, compassion and making sure that every day counts. Which is exactly what Carl does. When the local authorities try to send him off to a retirement home, Carl realises he has one chance left to do his best by his late wife, so he ties hundreds of helium-filled balloons to their home and floats the house out of the bustling city and across the tops of the clouds towards the place he and Ellie had always dreamed of visiting. 20 25

It's only when Carl is thousands of feet up that he gets a knock at the front door and realises he's brought an unexpected guest with him – a lovably useless local kid called Russell, who found himself on Carl's front porch when the house took off. Proud he'll be able to help navigate the journey using his **GPS tracker**, Russell throws his arms open enthusiastically, only to mistakenly lob the location gadget out of the window on to the clouds below.

30

'Oops', says Russell, as he and Carl watch the flying object hurtle away from them. And so the pair's adventure really begins.

From *The Guardian*, 17 March 2015

Vocabulary

aviator: flyer, pilot

GPS tracker: device which helps you locate your position via satellite

Spend 30 minutes on this section.

1 List **three** features or aspects of reviews that you can identify in this text.

_____   _____   _____   [1]

2 Look at the first paragraph (lines 1–6). In what year was the film first released?

_____ [1]

3 Look at lines 3–6. At what point in Carl and Ellie's life does the animation start?

_____ [1]

4 Look at the first paragraph. What adjective does the writer use in the first sentence that means 'surprising'?

_____ [1]

5 Look at line 1. What does the word 'classic' suggest about how people view the film now? Tick **one** answer.

A Old ☐

B Modern ☐

C Well-known ☐

D Unusual ☐ [1]

6 Look at lines 3–6. What does the adjective 'wide-eyed' suggest about the children?

_____ [1]

7 Look at line 4. The writer describes Carl and Ellie as 'button-nosed' children. What does the image suggest about their noses?

_____ [1]

8 What is the purpose of the first paragraph of the review?

Tick one answer.

A To give the writer's overall viewpoint about the film ☐

B To introduce the main character and their background ☐

C To reveal how the film ends and what happens to Carl ☐

D To tell the reader about the actors and the director ☐ [1]

9 Look at the second paragaraph (lines 7–12). Explain, in your own words, what the following phrase suggests about the effect the film has on the audience?

Up has you with this opening sequence and doesn't let you go.

_____

_____ [2]

10 Look at the second paragraph (lines 7–12). Explain why the writer lists events using commas rather than divide the sentence up into smaller sentences?

In quick succession, the two grow up, fall in love, get married and build a home together.

_____

_____ [2]

11 Look at the third paragraph (lines 13-17). Explain what the writer suggests about the film by using the adverbs 'heart-wrenchingly' and 'magically' in the following sentence.

*Yet, **magically**, despite **heart-wrenchingly** understated scenes like Ellie's death, Up is always one step ahead, making you laugh out loud just when you least expect it.*

   a 'magically' suggests _____

   b 'heart-wrenchingly' suggests _____ [2]

12 Look at the fifth paragraph. Rewrite the following sentence as three shorter sentences.

It's only when Carl is thousands of feet up that he gets a knock at the front door and realises he's brought an unexpected guest with him – a lovably useless local kid called Russell, who found himself on Carl's front porch when the house took off.

_____

_____

_____ [1]

13 Look at the article as a whole. What is the main tense the writer uses to describe what happens in the film?

_____ [1]

14 Rewrite the following sentence in your own words so that it is clear what the writer means.

Some films may try to tease out a tear at some point along the way and never quite achieve it.

Start: Some films might attempt to _____

_____ [2]

15 Throughout the review, the writer uses connectives to explain the plot.

   a Give one connective from the first paragraph that could be replaced with 'though'.

_____

b Give one time connective from the second paragraph that could be replaced by 'shortly' or 'shortly after'.

_____ [2]

16 You are going to sum up the main plot of the film as outlined in the review. Use the table to complete these notes.

Who Carl and Ellie are and their life together	
What happens to Carl after Ellie dies	
What happens when Carl and Russell meet	

[3]

17 Using the information in the notes, write a summary of the plot of _Up_. Write up to **50 words**. Use your own words as much as possible.

_____

_____

_____

_____ [2]

Section B: Writing

*Spend 45 minutes on this section in total. You may spend **15 minutes** planning your answer below.*

18 Write a review of any book or film that means a lot to you.

You could consider:

- what makes the book or film so special
- what you will include about the story/plot (without giving away the ending)
- what you will include about the characters and themes.

Write your plan here.

Now write your review on a separate sheet of paper. [25]

Test 6: FICTION: Poetry

This test is 90 minutes long (including 30 minutes of reading and planning time).

Section A: Reading

Spend 45 minutes on this section.

*Before you answer the test questions, spend **15 minutes** reading and making notes.*

Read the text.

As you are reading, note down your answers to the big five questions.

- Who is the poem about?

- What is happening in the poem?

- When are the events happening: now, in the past or in the future?

- Where do the events take place?

- Why has the writer written this poem?

(These notes are to help you prepare for the test. They will not be given marks.)

Night Flight

Tonight I fancy a flight,
so I shuffle my short feathers
and jump.

Clusters of city lights
stretch, spread and sprawl   5
into sparkling starfish.

A whisper of clouds
tickles my feet.
A current lifts me like a leaf –

I float, I glide,   10
I hold my feathered wings out wide
and watch the world beneath.

The occasional plane passes.
The odd meteorite. Together,
we set the sky alight.   15

Flight is always best at night.

                    By Laura Mucha

Spend 30 minutes on this section.

1 What features of poetry can you see in this text?

    1 It is divided into stanzas.

    2 _____

    3 _____

    4 _____ [1]

2 In the first stanza, when does the flight take place?

_____ [1]

3 Look at the first stanza. What verb means 'would like' or 'desire'?

_____ [1]

4 Look at the first stanza. Explain why the poet might have put 'and jump' on its own line.

_____ [1]

5 In the first stanza, the poet uses onomatopoeia. Give **one** word that is onomatopoeic.

_____ [1]

6 Look at the second stanza. What word does the writer use that means 'glittering' ?

_____ [1]

7 In the second stanza, the poet uses a metaphor. What two things does she bring together in her metaphor?

_____ [1]

8 Look at the second stanza. Find an example of alliteration. Write the lines.

_____ [1]

9 a Look at the third stanza. The lines 'A whisper of clouds / tickles my feet' mixes two senses together. Which two senses are they?

_____ [1]

  b What does this description suggest about the feeling of the clouds? Explain in one sentence.

_____ [2]

10 a Look at the third stanza. What simile does the speaker/poet use to describe what happens to her?

_____ [1]

b What does this tell us? Tick **two** answers.

A The wind is blowing. ☐

B She is falling from a tree. ☐

C She is very light. ☐

D She is heavy. ☐ [1]

11 Look at the fifth stanza. What word does the poet use to suggest that the speaker is united with the plane and the meteorite?

_____ [1]

12 Why does the poet say: 'Flight is always best at night'? Explain in one sentence.

_____ [1]

13 The poet uses a number of words and phrases from within the semantic field of 'flight' or 'flying'. Find **four** examples.

_____

_____ [2]

14 The poem is organised into six stanzas. What event in the first stanza tells the reader that this is the beginning of the flight?

_____ [1]

15 Look at the poem as a whole. Write two pairs of rhymes used by the poet.

Pair 1: _____ and _____

Pair 2: _____ and _____ [2]

16 The poet creates vivid effects.

a Select **one** quotation that suggests what the speaker sees is beautiful.

_____ [1]

b Select **one** quotation that suggests she is good at flying.

_____ [1]

17 What mood does the poet create in this poem? Tick **one** answer.

A Scary

B Magical

C Unpleasant

D Sad [1]

18 Explain your answer to Question 17 in 25–35 words, using at least one quotation from the poem.

_____

_____

_____ [2]

Section B: Writing

*Spend 45 minutes on this section. You may spend **15 minutes** planning your answer below.*

19 Write your own poem about flying.

Think about:

- how you can use the senses in your writing

- how the structure and organisation of the poem could help show your ideas

- how you can use sound and imagery to make your poem come to life.

Write your plan here.

Now write your poem on a separate sheet of paper. [25]

Test 5: Non-fiction

Self-assessment for Section A: Reading

Focus	Marks available	My score
Language and vocabulary	**Subtotal: 7**	
Understand literal meanings (Q4)	1	
Understand implicit meanings (Q5)	1	
Explain implicit meanings (Q6)	1	
Explain effects of word choice/linguistic, literary or dramatic techniques (Q9, Q11)	2, 2	
Text type, form, purpose and audience	**Subtotal: 3**	
Recognise/identify the writer's purpose/intended audience (Q8)	1	
Recognise the use of specific features/techniques (Q1, Q13)	1, 1	
Understanding ideas and content	**Subtotal: 10**	
Locate and retrieve information (Q2, Q3)	1, 1	
Take notes for a summary (Q16)	3	
Summarise information (Q17)	2	
Identify key issues or main points or themes (Q14)	2	
Identify mood/characterisation/relationships (Q7)	1	
Structure, grammar and punctuation	**Subtotal: 5**	
Recognise and/or comment on overall text structure (Q15)	2	
Recognise and/or comment on paragraph/scene/stanza structure (Q10)	2	
Recognise and/or comment on sentence/line structure (Q12)	1	
TOTAL	**25**	

What I did well: _____

_____

_____

What I can improve: _____

_____

_____

Test 5: Non-fiction

Self-assessment for Section B: Writing

Focus	Checklist	✓	Marks available	My score
Ideas, planning and content	I made a useful plan or structure.		5	
	I ensured my answer was relevant to the task, its audience and purpose.			
	I included key features of the text type/form.			
	I made my voice or viewpoint clear.			
Language and vocabulary	I used a range of vocabulary.		3	
	I used vocabulary precisely.			
	I used words and phrases for effect.			
	I used other language features or techniques for effect (like positive adjectives or adverbs).			
Grammar and punctuation	I used a range of sentence types accurately.		7	
	I used different sentence types for clarity or emphasis.			
	I used punctuation accurately.			
	I used punctuation to make meaning clear.			
	I used formal or informal language appropriately.			
Paragraphing and structure	I used organisational features (where relevant).		7	
	I used paragraphs accurately and to help structure my text.			
	I used a range of connectives to link ideas.			
Spelling	I checked my spelling was accurate.		3	
TOTAL			**25**	

What I did well: _____

_____

_____

What I can improve: _____

_____

_____

Test 6: Fiction

Self-assessment for Section A: Reading

Focus	Marks available	My score
Language and vocabulary	**Subtotal: 6**	
Understand literal meanings (Q3, Q6)	1, 1	
Understand implicit meanings (Q9a)	1	
Recognise/identify linguistic or literary techniques (Q5, Q7, Q8)	1, 1, 1	
Text type, form, purpose and audience	**Subtotal: 7**	
Recognise/identify the use of specific features/techniques (Q1, Q10a, Q15)	1, 1, 2	
Explain the writer's use of specific features/techniques for a text type/form/purpose/audience (Q9b, Q10b)	2, 1	
Understanding ideas and content	**Subtotal: 10**	
Locate and retrieve information (Q2, Q11)	1, 1	
Recognise/identify key issues or main points or themes (Q13)	2	
Recognise/identify mood, characterisation/relationships (Q16a, Q16b, Q17)	1, 1, 1	
Comment on or explain how the writer creates mood, characters or relationships (Q12, Q18)	1, 2	
Structure, grammar and punctuation	**Subtotal: 2**	
Recognise and/or comment on overall text structure (Q4, Q14)	1, 1	
TOTAL	**25**	

What I did well: _____

_____

_____

What I can improve: _____

_____

_____

Test 6: Fiction

Self-assessment for Section B: Writing

Focus	Checklist	✓	Marks available	My score
Ideas, planning and content	I made a useful plan or structure.		5	
	I ensured my answer was relevant to the task, its audience and purpose.			
	I included key features of the text type/form.			
	I made my voice, mood or viewpoint clear.			
Language and vocabulary	I used a range of vocabulary.		7	
	I used vocabulary precisely.			
	I used words and phrases for effect.			
	I used other language features or techniques for effect (like imagery).			
	I used formal or informal language appropriately.			
Layout and organisation	I considered and used an overall shape or form to support my ideas.		5	
	I used punctuation to make meaning clear.			
	I used verses or stanzas to organise or draw attention to my ideas.			
Sound and rhythm	I used repetition for effect or meaning.		5	
	I used rhythm and/or rhyme for effect.			
	I used specific words or phrases because of their sound.			
Spelling	I checked my spelling was accurate.		3	
TOTAL			**25**	

What I did well: _____

_____

_____

What I can improve: _____

_____

_____

End of Year Assessment 1: Non-fiction

This test is 1 hour 10 minutes long.

Section A: Reading

Spend 40 minutes on this section.

*Spend 10 minutes reading **Text A** and **Text B** and 30 minutes answering the questions in this section.*

*Read **Text A** and answer questions 1–8 below.*

Text A

Visit Japan

BLOG HOME   ABOUT ME   LINKS   ARCHIVE

20 Reasons Why You Should Visit Japan

Japan is the most amazing tourist destination and it offers many unique experiences that you cannot find in any other part of the world. The culture of this country is an interesting blend of Eastern traditions and Western modernity that can be seen everywhere […].

1. Pristine natural scenery   5

The first reason to visit is obviously the natural beauty of the country. Even though many people think of Japan as a highly modern country with flashy neon lights and advanced technology, shopping malls and high-end stores, there are many ways in which Japan is a nature lover's paradise as well!

As soon as you travel outside of the big and modern cities, you will discover   10
that the country is home to some of the best natural scenery in the world.
From the wilderness in Hokkaido to the white pristine beaches of Okinawa,
Japan's nature is incredibly diverse. The rugged mountains, rocky coastlines,
pristine white beaches, bamboo forests and some of the world's most beautiful
waterfalls are just some of the natural beauty to be enjoyed all year round.   15

2. Mount Fuji

Mount Fuji is famous all over the world as a place to visit during any season
of the year. But the majestic Fujisan is not 'just a mountain' as it takes a very
special, sacred place in the Japanese culture. Since the 7th century it has been
a sacred site for Shintoism, the indigenous religion of Japan. Japanese people   20
have always held Mount Fuji close to their heart and Mount Fuji is displayed in
many artistic outings, including (ancient) pottery, calligraphy, ukiyo-e paintings
and woodblock prints.

Climbing Mount Fuji is at the top of many people's bucket list and an estimated
400,000 people climb the volcano each year. The climbing season of the   25
highest peak (3,776 m) in Japan lasts from early July to early September.
Though, even if you are not keen on making your way to the summit, Mount
Fuji is a sight to behold.

From the Japan Wonder Travel Blog

1 What is the purpose of this extract? Tick **one** answer.

A To inform ☐

B To advise ☐

C To explain ☐

D To persuade ☐ [1]

2 Look at the first sentence of paragraph two. Which word does the writer use to emphasise how clear it is that Japan is a good tourist destination?

_____ [1]

3 What techniques does the writer use to guide the reader through the extract?
Give **two** techniques.

_____ [1]

4 Look at line 3. What does the word 'blend' suggest about the culture of Japan?

_____ [1]

5 Explain why the writer used the word 'Pristine' in the subheading for paragraph two.

_____ [1]

6 Look at the second paragraph (lines 6–9). Which phrase in the following sentence suggests that Japan can be enjoyed by nature lovers, despite also being modern.

Even though many people think of Japan as a highly modern country…

_____ [1]

7 Look at the fourth paragraph. Read the second sentence (lines 18–19). Why do you think the writer uses the word 'majestic' to describe Mount Fuji?

_____ [2]

8 a Look at line lines 20–23. Read the sentence beginning 'Japanese people have always held Mount Fuji close to their heart'.

What type of literary device is the phrase 'close to their heart'?

_____ [1]

b What do we learn about Mount Fuji from the fact that climbing the mountain is 'at the top of many people's bucket list' (line 24)?

_____ [1]

*Read **Text B** and answer questions 9–18.*

Text B

The Ultimate Guide to the Cherry Blossom Festival in Japan (2023)

The humble cherry blossom has been an important part of Japanese culture for centuries. Today, visitors come from all over the world to join in the celebrations that mark the beginning of spring, while admiring the delicate pink cherry blossoms known as 'sakura'.

What Is the Cherry Blossom Festival? 5

Japan's famous cherry blossom festival season begins around the end of March and lasts for approximately 2 weeks, depending on location. Cherry trees can bloom right through until May the further north you travel, so dedicated sakura viewers can head north to enjoy even more sakura spotting.

Top viewing spots like Maruyama Park, Mount Yoshino, Himeji Castle, and 10
Fuji Five Lakes are some of the most atmospheric places in the world and are wonderful places to see the beautiful blooms. For those who would like to enjoy a more scaled-down celebration of spring, there are plenty of lesser-known viewing spots where visitors can picnic in peace.

The aristocrats of days gone by often wrote poetry or painted pictures to 15
celebrate the beauty of the cherry blossom. These days, viewings are more about eating, drinking, and coming together to celebrate the beginning of spring.

Public parks, rivers, and other attractions where cherry trees are found will fill up with the smell of barbecue, food stalls, and the sound of celebrations during the season. So popular are the seasonal festivities, it can be hard to find a space in 20
some of the more popular viewing locations.

Why Is the Cherry Blossom so Culturally Important in Japan?

The blossom viewing in Japan is believed to have first started in the Nara period of the country's history between 710 A.D. and 794 A.D. The ancient farmers also used the blooming of the sakura flowers to help them understand when the time 25
was right to plant their rice crops, helping to keep famine at bay.

Fast forward a few hundred years and the family members and the courtiers of the most important imperial families made it fashionable to hold gatherings to celebrate the occasion of the annual new bloom at the beginning of spring.

Traditionally, the Japanese have always believed that the cherry blossom 30
represents the fragility and the beauty of life and that every blossom is a reminder that life can also be tragically short. Even today, the newly emerging blossoms of the cherry trees are considered to be a representation of hope, beauty, and new life — all of which most definitely deserve to be celebrated.

From the Upgraded Points website, 9 August 2023

9 Look at lines 2–4. How does the reader know that this festival is very popular?

_____

_____ [1]

10 Look at the first paragraph (lines 1–4). Which word does the writer use to suggest that visitors find the blossoms very beautiful?

_____ [1]

11 Look at the second paragraph. The festival season is in March only. Tick true or false.

T [ ]   F [ ]   [1]

12 Look at lines 15–17. Why does the writer use the past tense to discuss the activities of aristocrats?

_____ [1]

13 Look at the fourth paragraph. Which phrase tells you that people's responses to the cherry blossom are different *now* compared to in the past?

_____ [1]

14 Look at lines 30–31. Explain what the writer means by 'cherry blossom represents the fragility […] of life'.

_____ [1]

15 Why does the writer use a dash in the final sentence of the extract?

_____ [1]

16 The writer suggests that the sakura create strong reactions in people. Explain how you can see this in the article, giving an example from the extract.

Quotation: _____

Explanation: _____ [2]

17 Look at Text A and Text B. They show how the Japanese people respond to places of natural beauty in a similar way. How do they respond? Give one piece of evidence from Text B to support your answer.

Answer: _____

Evidence: _____ [1]

18 a Imagine that you are going to write a letter advising a friend who plans to visit Japan for the cherry blossom festivals. Use the table below to make some notes from Text B.

Advice for a visit to the Cherry Blossom Festival	Notes
When to go	
Length of visit	
Places to go	
Things to do when there	
Things to bear in mind	

[3]

b Use the notes in the table to write a summary of your advice to a friend wanting to visit the Japanese blossom festivals. Write up to 50 words. Use your own words as much as possible.

_____

_____

_____

_____ [2]

Section B: Writing

Spend 30 minutes on this section.

19 Write an account of a visit to a festival or celebration for your school magazine.

You could include:

- the type of festival

- what you did at the festival

- what made the festival interesting/enjoyable

- whether or not you would advise others to go.

Write your plan here.

Now write your account on a separate sheet of paper.

[25]

End of Year Assessment 2: Fiction

This test is 1 hour and 10 minutes long.

Section A: Reading

Spend 40 minutes on this section.

Spend 10 minutes reading the text and 30 minutes answering the questions in this section.

Read this extract from a short story. The narrator has been looking forward to the Hinamatsuri Girls' Day Festival of the Dolls.

I wake up in a flash and am half out of bed before I open my eyes, or so it seems. Today is the day! I have been waiting for this for weeks. The preparations for Hinamatsuri are starting this very day, and I will finally get to see the **obina and mebina**, my special dolls which my grandparents have brought from Japan.

We don't normally celebrate Girls' Day and at 10 I'm almost too old for it. But I heard Mum arguing over the phone with **Sobo** and she insisted that the tradition should live on. I could hear her voice even though Mum was trying to hide in the other room. 5

'My granddaughter needs to know what it's like to be our princess for the day, to giggle with her friends and eat Cherry Blossom cookies. I might even make my Strawberry Daifuku! Her beautiful dolls have been sat here for years!' 10

I liked the sound of 'her dolls' and had secretly felt quite smug that there would be a special gift for me to play with that my brother might not want to 'borrow'.

I've lived in England all of my life (my parents made the journey here to study and never went back) and this is my grandparents' first visit to see us as we finally have a spare room. They arrived yesterday and since then the dining room has been out of bounds to all but my mum and Sobo who have been in and out in a frenzy with armfuls of stuff. I don't know what they're going to do with the old red curtains from my bedroom but I'm sure I've seen packets of pinkish sweets and bright strips of material hanging out of the endless plastic bags that Mum has been sneaking in for weeks. (They've been lurking in the bottom of her wardrobe where she thinks I haven't seen them... but nothing escapes my brother and me if there's the possibility of sweets being involved.) 15 20

'Morning, my little peach!' my grandmother sings out as I shuffle into the kitchen in my slippers.

'You'll be lucky to find a peach tree around here...' Grandfather grumbles as he reads the news online. 25

Mum has her back to me and is already surrounded by bowls of brightly coloured rice crackers, angled every which way like shark fins in a lagoon, mounds of rice and sushi papers, and a huge silvery fish basks in a shallow tray, its scales glinting under the worktop lights like flashing knives.

I grab a yoghurt out of the fridge and turn away. 30

'Don't get yoghurt on your new dress,' my mum, with eyes in the back of her head, yells. 'Mo, you've three hours until your friends arrive.'

Suddenly an idea pops into my head and I'm so excited I almost drop my spoon. The dolls! I can go and see the dolls. Surely they'll be laid out by now? Sobo has brushed away all of my questions since they arrived with their bulging luggage yesterday. She says the dolls have to be presented in some special way and I will see them when I see them. 35

Trembling, I creep, a hunting cat, towards the dining room, turning my head to the right and left dramatically, checking the coast is clear. No sign of Dad anywhere; maybe he's gone to fetch Kai from his sleepover. 40

I get to the dining room door and stealthily place my hand on the door handle. It's not usually shut, so I pull it down cautiously, ears peeled for the slightest creak or groan. Silently, the door opens, not even a whisper of wood on the fading blue carpet. The table isn't where it would usually be: it's pushed against the wall under the window.

I'm not really interested in that though. My eyes are distracted by red strings of brightly 45 coloured silk objects, each one tailed with tassels of all the colours in the rainbow. They hang from the ceiling, creating a curtain across the room. Silken babies, magnolia flowers and balls of different sizes hang from the ribbons of red that swing in the breeze from the door and I pause, heart pounding, in case there are bells on them to give away 50 my trespassing.

Pushing through the curtain, my eyes are drawn instantly to a multi-tiered construction, a bit like one side of a pyramid, except it is only head high and is draped in my red velvet curtains! My eyes flit to the top of the display, where two china figures sit in pride of place. They sit rigid, fixed on their ceramic cushions, surrounded by big fat skirts, their painted robes ugly glossy black and red. Below them on the lower tiers are many 55 smaller ceramic statues, almost as fancily dressed. But where are *my* dolls? I scrabble through the box of grey packing tissue left in the centre of the carpet, increasingly furious and frustrated.

'Those old things are my dolls? Those old things?'

Vocabulary

obina and mebina: traditional Japanese dolls used for display on Girls' Day

Sobo: Grandmother

1 Look at line 2. What is the effect of the simple sentence 'Today is the day!'? Tick the answer which most closely sums it up.

   A It adds a sense of excitement. ☐

   B It keeps the reader's attention. ☐

   C It is clearer. ☐

   [1]

2 Read paragraph two (lines 5–7). What does this paragraph reveal about why the grandmother wants the family to celebrate Girls' Day?

_____

_____ [2]

3 Look at line 11. What does it mean when it says she 'felt quite smug'?

_____ [1]

4 Look at line 12. Why is the word 'borrow' in inverted commas?

_____ [1]

5 Look at line 15. What does 'out of bounds' mean?

_____ [1]

6 Look at the quotation below (lines 20–21). Explain what you learn about Mo and her brother when you read it.

… but nothing escapes my brother and me if there's the possibility of sweets being involved.

_____ [2]

7 Look at the eighth paragraph. Why is the whole of this paragraph written as one sentence?

_____ [1]

8 Look at line 27. What are the connotations of the image 'like shark fins in a lagoon' that the writer uses to describe the rice crackers?

_____ [1]

9 Look at the eleventh, twelfth and thirteenth paragraphs (lines 33–44). How is Mo feeling during the events described? Choose **two** quotations to illustrate two different emotions.

Quotation	Emotion

[4]

10 Reread the fourteenth paragraph (lines 45–50). Explain how the writer lets us know that Mo is aware that she is doing something wrong. Include one quotation to support your answer.

_____

_____ [3]

11 Look at line 52. Which literary device does the writer use in the line 'a bit like one side of a pyramid'.

_____ [1]

12 Explain why Mo is so disappointed by the Hinamatsuri dolls.

_____ [3]

13 How has the writer structured this text? Select from the choices below. Tick as many as you think apply.

- Starts with a flashforward ☐

- Starts with a flashback ☐

- Chronological ☐

- Follows a traditional story arc towards a dramatic event ☐

- Follows a pattern where a hero shows a flaw and is punished ☐ [2]

14 a Tick the text features which this extract includes.

A Heading ☐

B Descriptive verbs and adjectives ☐

C Subheadings ☐

D Characters ☐

E Persuasive language ☐

F A sequence of events which create a narrative ☐

G Literary techniques, such as similes and metaphors ☐ [1]

b What type of text do you think this is?

_____ [1]

Section B: Writing

Spend 30 minutes on this section.

15 Write your own story about a receiving a gift.

You should consider:

- the setting – where and when the story takes place
- the characters – who the main character is
- the viewpoint – first person or third person?
- how the story develops – what the gift is, how it changes things.

Write your plan here.

Now write your story on a separate sheet of paper.

[25]

End of Year Assessment 1: Non-fiction
Self-assessment for Section A: Reading

Focus	Marks available	My score
Language and vocabulary	**Subtotal: 8 marks**	
Understand literal meanings (Q2, Q4)	1, 1	
Explain literal meanings (Q5)	1	
Understand implicit meanings (Q6)	1	
Explain implicit meanings (Q7)	2	
Identify linguistic or literary techniques (Q8a)	1	
Explain effects of literary techniques (Q14)	1	
Text type, form, purpose and audience	**Subtotal: 3 marks**	
Identify the writer's purpose (Q1)	1	
Explain the writer's use of specific techniques for a purpose/audience (Q8b)	1	
Comment on the author's viewpoint/argument (Q17)	1	
Understanding ideas and content	**Subtotal: 11 marks**	
Locate and retrieve information (Q11)	1	
Take notes for a summary (Q18a)	3	
Summarise information (Q18b)	2	
Recognise/identify key issues or main points or themes (Q9, Q10, Q13, Q16)	1, 1, 1, 2	
Structure, grammar and punctuation	**Subtotal: 3 marks**	
Comment on punctuation (Q15)	1	
Recognise presentational or organisational features (Q3)	1	
Comment on grammatical features (Q12)	1	
TOTAL	**25**	

What I did well: _____

_____

_____

What I can improve: _____

_____

_____

End of Year Assessment 1: Non-fiction

Self-assessment for Section B: Writing

Focus	Checklist	✓	Marks available	My score
Ideas, planning and content	I made a useful plan or structure.		5	
	I ensured my answer was relevant to the task, its audience and purpose.			
	I included key features of the text type/form.			
	I made my voice or viewpoint clear.			
Language and vocabulary	I used a range of vocabulary.		3	
	I used vocabulary precisely.			
	I used words and phrases for effect.			
	I used language features or techniques for effect.			
Grammar and punctuation	I used a range of sentence types accurately.		7	
	I used different sentence types for clarity or emphasis.			
	I used punctuation accurately to make meaning clear.			
	I used formal or informal language appropriately.			
Paragraphing and structure	I used organisational features (where relevant).		7	
	I used paragraphs accurately and to help structure my text.			
	I used a range of connectives to link ideas.			
Spelling	I checked my spelling was accurate.		3	
TOTAL			**25**	

What I did well: _____

_____

_____

What I can improve: _____

_____

_____

End of Year Assessment 2: Fiction

Self-assessment for Section A: Reading

Focus	Marks available	My score
Language and vocabulary	**Subtotal: 5 marks**	
Explain literal meanings (Q3, Q5)	1, 1	
Understand implicit meanings (Q6)	2	
Explain effects of literary techniques (Q8)	1	
Text type, form, purpose and audience	**Subtotal: 3 marks**	
Identify the text type (Q14b)	1	
Recognise/identify the use of specific features/techniques (Q11, Q14a)	1, 1	
Understanding ideas and content	**Subtotal: 12 marks**	
Recognise key issues or main points or themes (Q2)	2	
Comment on or explain how the writer creates mood, characters or relationships (Q9, Q10, Q12)	4, 3, 3	
Structure, grammar and punctuation	**Subtotal: 5 marks**	
Recognise overall text structure (Q13)	2	
Recognise and/or comment on sentence structure (Q1, Q7)	1, 1	
Comment on punctuation (Q4)	1	
TOTAL	**25**	

What I did well: _____

_____

_____

What I can improve: _____

_____

_____

End of Year Assessment 2: Fiction

Self-assessment for Section B: Writing

Focus	Checklist	✓	Marks available	My score
Ideas, planning and content	I made a useful plan or structure.		5	
	I ensured my answer was relevant to the task, purpose and form/genre.			
	I kept the reader interested.			
	I created a well-developed character.			
Language and vocabulary	I used a range of vocabulary.		3	
	I used vocabulary precisely.			
	I used words and phrases for effect.			
	I used literary techniques such as imagery.			
Grammar and punctuation	I used a range of sentence types.		7	
	I used different sentence types accurately.			
	I used punctuation accurately.			
	I used punctuation to make meaning clear.			
Paragraphing and structure	My story or description has a logical structure.		7	
	I used a range of sentence openings.			
	I used paragraphs accurately to develop the narrative.			
	I used a range of connectives to link ideas.			
Spelling	I checked my spelling was accurate.		3	
TOTAL			**25**	

What I did well: _____

_____

_____

What I can improve: _____

_____

_____

Acknowledgements

Texts

The publishers gratefully acknowledge the permissions granted to reproduce copyright material in the book. Every effort has been made to contact the holders of copyright material, but if any have been inadvertently overlooked, the publishers will be pleased to make the necessary arrangements at the first opportunity.

We are grateful to the following for permission to reproduce copyright material:

Extracts on pp.6 and 8 from *Jamaica Inn* by Daphne du Maurier, Virago, copyright © The Chichester Partnership, 1938. Reproduced by permission of Curtis Brown Ltd, London on behalf of The Chichester Partnership; An extract on p.24 from *Charlie and the Chocolate Factory* by Roald Dahl, Puffin Books, copyright © The Roald Dahl Story Company Limited, 1964. Reproduced by permission of David Higham Associates; and Puffin, an imprint of Penguin Young Readers Group, a division of Penguin Random House LLC. All rights reserved; An extract on p.41 from 'Fate' by Shi Tie-sheng, published in *The Picador Book of Contemporary Chinese Fiction*, Ed by Carolyn Choa and David Su Li-Qun, Picardor, 1998. Reproduced by permission of the publisher through PLSClear; An extract on pp.45–46 from 'How to stay safe from avalanches when ski-ing' by Lucy Aspden-Kean and Louise Hall in *The Telegraph*, 17/03/2023, copyright © Lucy Aspden-Kean and Louise Hall / Telegraph Media Group Limited 2023; An extract on p.51 from 'Caught in an avalanche' by Robert Seethaler, translated by Charlotte Collins in *A Whole Life*, Picador. 2015. Reproduced by permission of the publisher through PLSClear; An extract on p.62 from 'Moon on a rainbow shawl; Can We Talk about This?; Shivered – review' by Kate Kellaway, *The Guardian*, 18/03/2012, copyright © Guardian News & Media Ltd, 2023; An extract on pp.68–69 from 'The film that makes me cry – *Up*' by Tess Riley, *The Guardian*, 17/03/2015, copyright © Guardian News & Media Ltd, 2023; The poem on p.74 'Night Flight' by Laura Mucha, from *Dear Ugly Sisters*, Otter-Barry Books, copyright © Laura Mucha 2020. Reproduced by kind permission of the author and David Higham Associates; An extract on p.84 from '20 Reasons Why You Should Visit Japan' Japan Wonder Travel Blog, https://blog.japanwondertravel.com/reason-to-visit-japan-14343. Reproduced by permission; and an extract on p.85 from 'The Ultimate Guide to the Cherry Blossom Festival in Japan' by Amar Hussain, https://upgradedpoints.com/travel/japan-cherry-blossom-festival-guide/. Reproduced with permission.

In some instances, we have been unable to trace the owners of copyright material, and we would appreciate any information that would enable us to do so.

Images

The publishers wish to thank the following for permission to reproduce photographs.

p.18 Aedka Studio/Shutterstock; p.45 RAW-films/Shutterstock